GW01280679

BED OF SPHINXES
PHILIP LAMANTIA

City Lights Books
San Francisco

1997 by Philip Lamantia
All Rights Reserved
10 9 8 7 6 5 4 3 2 1

Cover design: Rex Ray
Book design: Nancy J. Peters
Typography: Harvest Graphics

Library of Congress Cataloging-in-Publication Data

Lamantia, Philip, 1927–
    Bed of sphinxes : selected poems / by Philip Lamantia.
        p.   cm.
    ISBN 0-87286-320-4 (pbk.)
    I. Title
PS3562.A42B43   1997
811'.54—dc20   96–9667
                                                                               CIP

City Lights Books are available to bookstores through our primary distributor: Subterranean Company, P.O. Box 160, 265 S. 5th St., Monroe, OR 97456. 541-847-5274. Toll-free orders 800-274-7826. FAX 541-847-6018. Our books are also available through library jobbers and regional distributors. For personal orders and catalogs, please write to City Lights Books, 261 Columbus Avenue, San Francisco, CA 94133.

CITY LIGHTS BOOKS are edited by Lawrence Ferlinghetti and Nancy J. Peters and published at the City Lights Bookstore, 261 Columbus Avenue, San Francisco, CA 94133.

Acknowledgments

Portions of this book were published in the following Philip Lamantia books:

>*Erotic Poems* (Bern Porter Books, Berkeley, 1946)
>*Touch of the Marvelous* (Oyez, Berkeley, 1966)
>*Ekstasis* (Auerhahn Press, San Francisco, 1959)
>*Destroyed Works* (Auerhahn Press, San Francisco, 1962)
>*Selected Poems 1943-1966* (City Lights Books,
>   San Francisco, 1967)
>*The Blood of the Air* (Four Seasons Foundation,
>   San Francisco, 1970)
>*Becoming Visible* (City Lights Books, San Francisco, 1981)
>*Meadowlark West* (City Lights Books, San Francisco, 1986)

The poems in the final section (Uncollected Poems) were originally published in *Arsenal, City Lights Review, Sulfur,* and *The Best American Poetry 1988.*

Contents

TOUCH OF THE MARVELOUS (1943-1946)

Touch of the Marvelous	1
Plumage of Recognition	3
Hermetic Bird	5
Automatic World	7
A Winter Day	9
A Civil World	11
The Enormous Window	13
Awakened From Sleep	15
Mirror and Heart	17
The Diabolic Condition	19
Infernal Landscape	21
I Am Coming	22
There Are Many Pathways to the Garden	23

FROM
EKSTASIS (1948-1958)

Inside the Journey	24
Animal Snared in His Revery	26
The Owl	27
[Man is in pain]	28
Terror Conduction	29
Dead Smoke	31
[What made tarot cards and fleurs-de-lis]	32
Interior Suck of the Night	34
[Iguana iguana]	35
Observatory	36
[As some light fell]	38
Sheri	39
[It's summer's moment in autumn's hour]	40
Ball	41
[In a grove]	42

FROM
DESTROYED WORKS (1958-1960)

Resurrections	43
Hypodermic Light	46
Fin del Mundo	51
The Wheel	53
Deamin	54
From the Front	56
Still Poems	58
Morning Light Song	61
High	62
Jeanlu	63
Infernal Muses	64
Subconscious Mexico City	65
Rompi	67

FROM
SELECTED POEMS (1963-1967)

Blue Grace	68
The Ancients Have Returned Among Us	70
She Speaks the Morning's Filigree	72
Voice of Earth Mediums	74
What Is Not Strange	75
Astro-Mancy	77
Coat of Arms	79

FROM
BLOOD OF THE AIR (1968-1970)

Blue Locus	81
The Talisman	82
Luminous	83
Ephemeris	85
Out of My Hat of Shoals	86
The Analog	87
Fantast	88
Horse Angel	89
Flaming Teeth	90

FROM
BECOMING VISIBLE (1971-1981)

The Romantic Movement	95
Bed of Sphinxes	97
Primavera	99
Becoming Visible	100
In Yerba Buena	101
Oraibi	103
Ultima Thule	105
Beyond This Trail of Crystal Rails	106
To Begin *Then* Not Now	107
Time Travelers Potlatch	108

FROM
MEADOWLARK WEST (1982-1986)

Words I Dream	109
There	110
Phi	111
Isn't Poetry the Dream of Weapons	112
Wilderness Sacred Wilderness	115
Native Medicine	117
America in the Age of Gold	118
Shasta	122

UNCOLLECTED POEMS (1985-1992)

Poem for André Breton	125
Ex-Cathedra	126
Unachieved	128
Diana Green	132
Egypt	137
Passionate Ornithology Is Another Kind of Yoga	140

| Index of titles, first lines | 142 |

Touch of the Marvelous

The mermaids have come to the desert
they are setting up a boudoir next to the camel
who lies at their feet of roses

A wall of alabaster is drawn over our heads
by four rainbow men
whose naked figures give off a light
that slowly wriggles upon the sands

I am touched by the marvelous
as the mermaids' nimble fingers go through my hair
that has come down forever from my head
to cover my body
the savage fruit of lunacy

Behold the boudoir is flying away
and I am holding onto the leg of the lovely one
called beneath the sea
BIANCA
She is turning
with the charm of a bird
into two giant lips
and I am now falling into the goblet of suicide

She is the angelic doll turned black
she is the child of broken elevators
she is the curtain of holes
that you never want to throw away

she is the first woman and the first man
and I am lost to have her

I am hungry for the secrets of the sadistic fish
I am plunging into the sea

I am looking for the region
where the smoke of your hair is thick
where you are again climbing over the white wall
where your eardrums play music
to the cat that crawls in my eyes
I am recalling memories of you BIANCA

I am looking beyond the hour and the day
to find you BIANCA

Plumage of Recognition

A soul drenched in the milk of marble
goes through the floor of an evening
that rides lost on a naked virgin
It gains power over the dull man:
it is a soul sucked by lepers

What liquid hour shall rivet
its song on my cat
with the neck of all space?

Morning and I may lose
the terrible coat of ill feeling
that has curled me into a chained dragon
the flower bursting with eyelids

Ah! a fever the skeleton of arson!
comes to rest on the citadel of the immortals
the diadem flickers and dies away
while running toward the vat of salted babies

They are creeping upon the wall my dagger
they are bulging with cradles
the era of the lunatic birds has arrived!

They have come to rape the town
infested with iron-blood clerks
and to send the hairless priests
down to the pool of deadly anchors

Parades are the enchantment of a brain
piled up like the water of an ocean
I enjoy the creation of a human table
to be in the center of the delirious crowd

There are birds perched on my bones
that will soon flood the avenues
with their serpent-like feathers
I am at a house built by Gaudí
"May I come in?"

Hermetic Bird

This sky is to be opened
this plundered body to be loved
this lantern to be tied
around the fangs of your heart

Lost on a bridge
going across oceans of tragedy
across islands of inflammable virgins
I stand
with my feathers entangled in your navel
with my wings opalescent in the night
and shout words heard tomorrow
in a little peasant cart
of the seventeenth century

Breath by breath
the vase in the tomb
breaks to give birth to a roving Sphinx
Tremble, sweet bird, sweet lion
hunger for you
hunger for your mother

The children in the lamps
play with our hair
swinging over the void

Here is a landscape on fire
Here are horses wet by the sour fluid of women

On the pillars of nicotine
the word *pleasure* is erased by a dog's tongue
On the pillars the bodies are opened by keys
the keys are nailed to my bed
to be touched at dawn
to be used in a dream

If one more sound is heard
the children will come out to murder
at the bottom of the lake
at the bottom of the lake

If the children murder
the owls will bleed
the wanton humans
who parade in basements of the sun

When the columns fall into the sea
with a crash involving prophecies and madmen
together in a little cradle
lifted into the robes of desire
and with our mouths opened for the stars
howling for the castles to melt at our feet
you and I
will ride over the breasts of our mother
who knows no one
who was born from unknown birds
forever in silence
forever in dreams
forever in the sweat of fire

Automatic World

The sun has drowned
virgins are no more
there is no need for understanding
but there is so much to see

So come with me
down the boulevard
of crawling veins
Don't be afraid
blood is cheap!

A paradise song?
A dirty story?
A love sonnet?
Scream it out!
Then we'll have the human walls
tumbling down to meet our march
into the raw-meat city!

The velvet robes are strewn
across the landscape
We step upon the sidewalk
that goes up and down
up to the clouds
down to the starving people
Don't ask me what to do!
Keep on going
we'll end up somewhere fast
on the moon perhaps!

Rainbow guns are dancing
in front of the movie queens
Everyone is laughing
flying dying
never knowing when to rest
never knowing when to eat

And the fountains come falling
out of her thistle-covered breasts
and the dogs are happy
and the clowns are knifing
and the ballerinas are eating stone

O the mirror-like dirt
of freshly spilt blood
trickling down the walls
the walls that reach the stars!

O the flock of sheep
breaking their flesh open
with bones sucked
from the brothels!

O the grave of bats
sailing through shops
with the violent hands!

When will these come?
When will these go?

The sun is riding into your eye
virgins are bursting
from under my flaming palms
and we are slowly floating away

A Winter Day

In the rose creeping into the tower of exiles
when the buffet is laden with jewels
when the night is filled with hate
when the womb of Eros is deserted
when the sleeping men are awakened
when the old lovers are no longer frightened
—my heart

The old women come down playing on the lawns
of the intangible murderers
the women are mine
Your eye is so smooth in the sunlight
you are no longer a child
you are old
spider of the blind
insolent mother
Do you care for my young hair
I want to lay the fibers of my heart over your face

It is a strange moment
as we tear ourselves apart in the silence
of this landscape
of this whole world
that seems to go beyond its own existence

You roll so beautifully over my bones
that have shaken off the flesh of their youth
My nakedness is never alarming
it is this way I adore you

Your hands with crystals shining into the night
pass through my blood
sever the hands of my eyes

We have come to a place where the nightingales sleep
We are filling up the oceans and the plains
with the old images of our phosphorescent bones

A Civil World

In a moment their faces will be visible.
You shall see the women who walk in a night of offensive sunlight that cuts through their cardboard thighs.
As the street is cleaned by the presidents of the nation, I can see the bowlegged men moving over to copulate with the maniacs.

As a rose runs down an alley, a purple nugget, giving off some blood, is suspended in air.
The children who are ten feet tall are wet.
Their faces are scorched, their eyes cut by glass.
They play their games as a steeple topples, as a clown's laugh is heard in church.
Quietly the mothers are killing their sons; quietly the fathers are raping their daughters.

But the women.

The eye wanders to a garden in the middle of the street.
There are poets dipping their diamond-like heads in the luminous fountain. There are grandmothers playing with the delicate toys of the chimera. There are perfumes being spilt on the garbage. There is a drunken nun flying out of a brothel.

The women are all colors.
Their breasts open like flowers, their flesh spreads over the park like a blanket. Their hair is soaked in the blood of their lovers, those who are the mirrors of this night.

The naked lovers! All of them, fifteen years old! One can still see their hair growing! They come from the mountains, from the stars even, with their handsome eyes of stone. Ah, these somnambulistic lovers, with their bellies full of arrows!

After the street has recaptured its loneliness, a precious stone casts its light on the perambulator I am to enter. One perambulator in the center of a world. A poet—far away in the mountains—can be heard chanting like an ape. I wonder when he will stop.

The Enormous Window

Within closets filled with nebulae
the bloodshot eyes
swim upward for the sun

This world of serpents and weeping women
is crushed in the violence
of a swamp large enough to contain
the enormous razor blade of the night

> *In the tropics*
> *the doctors prescribe*
> *sand for the heart*
>
> *Ad astra*
> *Ad astra*

With fire spitting across the horizon
and like a little flake of flesh
bashed against our heads
midnight seeps through the marigolds
in the garden no longer quiet
as corpses float through its arbor of palm trees

Neurasthenics
with young blood
ride to the stars
with horses from Peru

> *Tomorrow evangelists*
> *the following day toys fall in love*
> *the last moment brings rabid boys*
> *beating their fathers with lightning rods —*
>
> *Ad Astra*
> *Ad Astra*

In the sea the clown of windows
encounters swift rocks
climbing upon his body
to rub against his wooden anus

As the jungle disappears
one theater of war gives birth to another
The bleeding eyes of murder
fall into the sea of this night

The performance begins
in the palm of your hand
where the swords mark the spot
where your eardrums take wings
to gather strength between two girls
raped at sunrise

Through the ceiling I can see beggers
walking on hands and knees
to reach a pyramid flung into the storm
where serpents drink champagne
and wash their women with the blood of prophets

The stars are wet tonight
the naked schoolmasters
are no longer in the gardens of childhood
and the sea has been heated for lions

And now you can bleed fire from statues
and the lower you descend into this bottomless pit
the higher will you rise
beyond the raped girls
beyond the wounded boys
trapped in the labyrinth
of their mother's hair
    beyond the soiled curtain of space

Awakened From Sleep

Swept from the clouds
we are among gardens under the sea.
Flaming white windows
from which nightingales flaunt in the sun.

Have we come from the cities of the plain
or the moon's lake of demons?

Your whole body is a wing,
daughter of half-seen worlds
together we fly to rocks of flesh
beneath the ashes of ancient lovers.

There is no rule here
no seasons and no misery
There are only our desires
revealed in the mist.
Here ghosts are reborn every moment
in the spider webs of your face.

Your hair is mingled with little children
laughing in the moonlight
butterflies have come to rest upon your lips
whose words clothe the dancing stars
falling lightly to earth.

You have become so monumental
and I so sleepy.
Water is trickling down your lucid breasts.

In a minute you'll be a shadow
and I a flame in sleep.

We'll meet
corridors will open
the rain will come in
the hot bite of dogs will be upon us.
And drifting with a marvelous touch
of all the moons of space
   will be the lovers
diffusing their blood
in the secret passageways of the heart.

Mirror and Heart

The teacups shattered upon the legs of ancient lovers
become a statue in Rome before you
my embittered gypsy

Pluck your feathers
stain the wings that carry your heart among assassins
Watch through the boudoir the satin shirts of drunken men
who have seen their poisoned hair scattered in fire
watch and regret nothing

Your fate is to follow the sleeping women
in the castle of memory with its smoked oceanic rocks
covered by blood and snow

Your body reclaiming the stars
lifts itself in a wooden frame
to be seen in boulevards
that twist themselves at dawn into my room

Advance with caution
as with locust in your belly
make a window that will follow the trees into a lake

Each bridegroom shall inherit a laugh of childhood
that will announce the coming of my felons
soft with murder
soft with your feathers growing upon their hands

The noiseless girl who places the eyes of her lover
in a glass of wine
is only a flower set between the oars of a boat
to petrify and to be sucked for blood

Don't be frightened my dark one
this dream that winds its way
against a mask worn by the first suicide
will fade away into another's fury
when the morning wears your torn dress

Awakened at the side of this hunted slave
your hands will whisper my name into the sands

As your lips raise water from the mist
an apparition of your mirror
takes you within its warmth
reflecting black wounds set open by the fingernail of the dumb

Solitude is your violence

Your burnt face is fading into the dream

My love
my gypsy
among the fallen you are luminous
You wander with those who are mystery
with a naked heart upon your breast

The Diabolic Condition

As the women who live within each other's bodies
descend from their polar regions
to the circle of demons
I become ready to offer myself to the smooth red snakes
    entwined in the heads of sorcerers

Between the black arms coming over the swamp
rushing to embrace me
and the distant sun in which abide the men who hold
    within their fists the Evil Eyes
between the tombs and beds of boneless magicians
who have worked in the secrecy of abandoned towers
despite my body flying away
despite the lizards who crawl into the altars where
    the potents are being prepared
despite the intrusion of doctors' maids
    and egyptologists
despite the old Doric temple carried in by the art lovers
despite the nest of mad beggars
the chant is heard
and the words of the chant are written in oceanic gardens

The flat walls are singing goodbye
we have entered the city where the dead masters speak to us
    of catacombs and the horned enchantress of Africa
The incantation is following us into the streets
and into the sky
We are ascending to the limitless cosmos of architecture
we are crawling backward to enormous hearts
that leap over the snow to climb into our bodies

Come my ritual wax and circles
my rose spitting blood
When the day is lit up by our magic candles
and the hours yell their sadistic songs and suck hard
into the night when the cats invade our skulls
then we will know the destructive ones have gone
out into the world to watch the cataclysm begin
as the final wave of fire pours out from their hearts

Infernal Landscape

A window that never ends
where infant eyes are unhooked
from the paper clown
who stands on a shattered mirror
picking rocks from his heart

In the absence of light
pulled through mist
my eyes are imprisoned
And the sun has regained its lions
whose flesh covers the earth
who know solitude is a flavor
of the polar night

But it is a criminal hand
that obscures the shadow of clowns
and the skeleton of solitude
It is this hand hiding in smoke
of burnt flesh
kissed and rekissed, sucked of flames
that is consumed in lust
A hand that grows of its own accord
giving thunder to sleep
as moonlight like a sword cuts through
its bracelet of animal entrails

Eyelids open as mouths
nourishing the criminal hand
Its fingers play upon water from thighs
whose serpents plunge into my body

Sand passes in the heart of the hand
as diamonds in a lake

I Am Coming

I am following her to the wavering moon
to a bridge by the long waterfront
to valleys of beautiful arson
to flowers dead in a mirror of love
to men eating wild minutes from a clock
to hands playing in celestial pockets
and to that dark room beside a castle
of youthful voices singing to the moon.

When the sun comes up she will live at a sky
covered with sparrow's blood
and wrapped in robes of lost decay.

But I am coming to the moon
and she will be there in a musical night
in a night of burning laughter
burning like a road of my brain
pouring its arm into the lunar lake.

There Are Many Pathways to the Garden

If you are bound for the sun's empty plum
there is no need to mock the wine tongue
but if you are going to a rage of pennies
over a stevedore's wax ocean
then, remember: all long pajamas are frozen dust
unless an axe cuts my flaming grotto.

You are one for colonial lizards
and over bathhouses of your ear
skulls shall whisper
of a love for a crab's rude whip
and the rimless island of refusal shall seat itself
beside the corpse of a dog
that always beats a hurricane
in the mad run for Apollo's boxing glove.

As your fingers melt a desert
an attempt is made to marry the lily-and-fig-foot dragon
mermaids wander and play with a living cross
a child invents a sublime bucket of eyes
and I set free the dawn of your desires.

The crash of your heart
beating its way through a fever of fish
is heard in every crowd of that thirsty tomorrow
and your trip ends in the mask of my candle-lit hair.

Inside the Journey

Quickly, I rocked between waves. Quickly, I got the god on the wing. Quickly, I picked the tarn from the twirling top. Quickly and quickly, and faster, faster: for the kill of the body's anger, for the win of the lost child, for the fall of wizards through revolving sheets of snow.

And so I walked all the streets become one street among the renegades who go unmolested, half-asleep, to the gardens of childhood—in the largest of a white love once a pink, pearl-shaped object on the horizon of their longing; a white love in a black space—no time in the land of nothing but time.

And this was my dream that lasted from some dawn to some midnight in the fallingdown room overlooking the oldest graveyard of Manhattan:

>   the poisonous stars: *benign*
>   the rootless tree: *nailed to the sky*
>   the black pit: *enclosing ladders of white light*
>   the icebergs of the mind: *floating to the tropics . . .*

For a long time I saw no other sky than the ceiling of this room where, from a chink of plaster, hung the image of paradise I embarked for like a ship to the Orient. I could hardly move my head. I could hardly say the word to ask for water. I could hardly conceive of *another* life. I threw the hex down, I swallowed the spells, I put the tumult down. If I spoke I would violate the wonder of that silence. If I moved, I would break across space like a knife cutting cheese. I knew all the constellations of infinite duration where my thoughts that flew away one day waited like brides for their bridegrooms of the infinite.

In another time, I was making blueprints for the Eternal, but the work was interrupted by some ogre who jumped out from behind a slab of magenta sky, and I was mesmerized on the spot between the poison I was wiping from my lips and the face behind the face I saw looking at me from the sky I was using as a mirror.

Anyway, I broke the spell. But another wave of invented emotions sank and another light fell on the crest of the wave: escape was a door I kept shutting all around me AND on those who were carving me, symbolically they said, for the first course at the restaurant for the initiates of the lake of love—which is to say, sperm ran high that year, breaking over the brains of those who know how to conduct themselves properly in *this* world: which is to say, life goes on gathering wool for the mothers of all the daughters whose tongues spit live lobsters and whose insatiable desire for some sea-salt paradise makes thunder break in my skull: which is to say, very simply and without metaphor, that my brain was oppressing me.

—And that is not the most of it—for I took a look into the great vacuum of *this* world, in order that the journey in space of that life that puts poetry to shame, since it strained at the risk of all my senses becoming nil and hurtled me further into abysmal giddiness, would terminate at the junction where I might be able to move while in a state of suspended animation, since if I did not move in the vacuum the vacuum would move within me. And this movement of what is lusting to annihilate the sense of life (instigating panic in the mind, heart and liver) and taking its place, therefore, within life itself—would only lead to my ejection from *this* world.

It is this Vacuum that makes possible that daily hell kept going to decimate the scapegoat inhabitants of the earth, inspiring nothing but apathy and further pollution, revolving on the sexual hydra—at one pole—and fed through the swine mongering mobs at the other pole, in order to do away with the memory of what WAS or MIGHT BE—and as I opened to IT I saw its Body that is a vast machinery, in perpetual motion, for the sole consumption of a certain kind of etherealized excrement transmuted out of the bestial layers of the human condition become entirely the cretinized image of God with whom, be it added, this machine copulates perpetually . . .

Animal Snared in His Revery

He breathes through his wounds.
The herbs that would heal him decay in the labyrinth of his great paw.
The sun sends medicinal currents to the wobbling island under his sunken tooth.
With agates of rain, the sibylline garden (oracles speak from the flowers) conceives grimly poisonous minerals traveling the earth veins.
The animal, blackening the light with an orb of his blood, reads on the televised leaves:
— SLEEP TERRORS RAGING —
— EXIT FROM DREAMS —
. . . and the green mouth cracks open underground.

The Owl

I hear him, see him — interpenetrate
those shadows warping the garden pathways,
as the dark steps I climb are lit up
by his Eye magnetic to the moon,
his Eye magnetic to the moon.

I have not seen him when windows are mute
to whisper his name; on that moment
erroneous bats slip out through the sky.
His lair conceives my heart,
all hearts make the triangle he uses for a nose,
sniffing bloodways to my brain:
the bloodways are lit up by his Eye.

On a sudden appearance he tortures leaves,
flays branches and divides segments
the sun has drawn. I do not falter
— in the dark he fortifies.
His color is *green,* green
to distend him over the earth.
He does not fly.
You meet him while walking.

He is not easily enticed to manifestation,
but stony silence, petrified moments
— a transfiguration — will bring him out,
focused on the screen where all transfigured bodies are.
You must be humble to his fangs
that paw the moonball dissolving in the space
from the corner of your eye:
he will trick you otherwise
— into daylight, where you meet his double while running.

By night, the deltas of the moon-spilled planet
are stoned under his wriggling light.

By day, he chokes the sun.

[Man is in pain]

Man is in pain
    ten bright balls bat the air
    falling through the window
    on which his double leans a net the air made
    to catch the ten bright balls

Man is a room
    where the malefic hand turns a knob
    on the unseen unknown double's door

Man is in pain
    with his navel hook caught on a stone quarry
    where ten bright balls chose to land
    AND where the malefic hand carves
        on gelatinous air THE WINDOW
    to slam shut on his shadow's tail

    Ten bright balls bounce into the unseen
    unknown double's net
Man is a false window
    through which his double walks to the truth
    that falls as ten bright balls
    the malefic hand tossed into the air

Man is in pain
    ten bright spikes nailed to the door!

Terror Conduction

The menacing machine turns on and off

Across the distance light unflickers active infinities

Under the jangling hand set going in the brain
                        THE WOMAN
menacing by white lacerations
                THE MAN
menacing
in a timeweighed fishbowl of the vertical act

and the woman and the man menacing together
                        out of mutual crucifixions
disgorge
      towers for the dead

              the woman menacing
the man menacing
the woman and the man menacing together
                BUT
THE CROWDS
      THE CROWDS MENACING
as eyes take off for NOTHINGNESS
in night rememorizing the primal menace
on a day in a night crossed with butchering
polite squeals humdrum
                  WHAT are all these
   wayward-looking   scorching   haggard
                 grim
perilous   witchlike   criminal
              SUBLIME

    drunken   wintered
                    GRAZING
  FACES
        FACES
              going by
like icebergs
        like music
                like boats
                        like mechanical toys
LIKE
    RAINING
           SWORDS!

Dead Smoke

Ambivalent miles, sorceries played, we drank from hatred's lake
Giant jades emanated spells, I played the windows of Hell
Perfumed birds out of emblematic halls
cut fire in two — caves yawned walls, cries, tigers
a mile below Saturn
presence of damnation
Shades in the meadow enlightened the cows
who made the walk of seas go round
and legends, iron stalks in the forest, carved the geometries
                                                    of Azoth

Winds have not flown longer than time we stopped
whose sail hit the rooms where you looked into voids
— a beast on a star, Crab on the moon, the sunken tooth —
Stalks of madness tripled fire
and sent gardens under the sea
mountains fell   dogs howled
You — O dark side of the moon —
interlaced light — shadows went on the water —
undeciphered glyphs, stones of the immortals — trophies
                                                    bled in gold

[What made tarot cards and fleurs-de-lis]

What made tarot cards and fleurs-de-lis
    chariots my heart to shackled towers
The priestess maps apocalypses
   Swords catch on medused hair
      Mandolins woman in a garden

They scaled the wall, they fell from a wall
Fleurs-de-lis illuminated on an eyeball
    came out of the wall

    they fought in a flower.

Symbologies systematized from sweat suctionings
made theatrical cruelty extend souls on a pensive
cloud turn   turning incendiary incentives ON

      They came to PEACE
and wailed in gavottes
   monsters cooled their mothers
in bubbling craters
         angels
  dropt leprous booty
On a high-flung season they blackened blood
             climbing the walls

A fleur-de-lis on a charging horse swam up
  into the moon-clad Knight
his lady on a wall
        raped
          moon-struck by wands
clapt in a bell, his lady shook fleurs-de-lis on the wind

                    Mandolins
            in a bile-styled peace
                            explode
        Knights go scattering swords
The Tripled Queen on a resinous wall
                        apparitioned
as fleurs-de-lis
                luminescent
            under burnt-out flesh
suddenly galed
                TAROTED
on medieval   stained   glass

Interior Suck of the Night

    Narcotic air
    simple as a a cone
    spun
    interior suck of the night

        bloodshot eyes of my genii
As the first branch of clouds hang for the infinite
I go across streets with candles aimed for lost windows
your NOTHING engraved on a cherry-button heart
your smile folding over the tables of the law

      Opium
              in a butterfly's dream
      windows open on broken stem of pipe
        chimes, cuneiforms
   of the marvelous and you, my innocent.
a shadow encrusted on a light beam
your eyes
        the daughters of your eyes
I see the salt spoon of the sibyl's you cooked
my hair my threads my nails with

[Iguana Iguana]

Iguana iguana
a giant slime lizard stuck to a wall

Cacti razored the night by candlelight
on ladders weeping to the moon

Antique music old music
fell from a rock-jagged temple
into the throat of Indian prayer wound
around the Virgin beyond the black box
they carried in Cristero
      with the beards of Don Quixote on.

Observatory

      Smoke
tilts in space
    sylphonic
downward
   into an appearance
  a beast a myth
  an intelligence
where are edges and limits
   —you are instigations—
hallucinates or realizes
and fires peremptory images

      Love
snaked by
    thru multi
  multitudinous Void
equals Death

      What permanency, Air
invigorator from sylphs, mercurial
spirits, geologic geometers
   PLACE
of initiates initiating occult pacts
zohars whose one book sealed
    in mythological golds
UNTOUCHABLE
    SPRINGS OPEN

   It's zenith
zodiacal beasts phospher
and stars devoured white

        Cosmical games are wars
not deciphered
        shift spaces O essence of smoke
not less black
        a being
        a world
        a sign

"YOU DO NOT CHART MY REGIONS"

Masks are not clouds
under the air speak
"I am rivers riven Zoltecs lightninged
what sleeps awakens geomancies of no metal"

[As some light fell]

    As some light fell
on the inscaped facade
    stains of interior cancer
          intervined the stars

    bewitched by time, a long room
of rooms who opened on you
              I
              R
              I
              S
the street corner flew into Spring
      ,precisely a lily or an iris—

Sheri

                    I walked you
                 sank you in black glass
              the trouble with the stars is
            they're too far from my eyes to yours
             First Wing and last pages of the albatross
       I   satellited   you   cocktails on   a   petrified   face
    The   l i q u e f a c t i o n   of the walls of the city
         For the Lord made all things   green
              opal eye,   lice,   dung
                  for jazz, green is the essence
                        of the lightfooted CLOSE UP
    like a mandolin sneaking up to you
                     Beatrixed and
                              marveled
                                    on FORTUNA'S GATE

[It's summer's moment in autumn's hour]

It's summer's moment in autumn's hour.
I walk over a carpet of leaves
Fallen on a hill overlooking the city
Watching the clouded moon cut
Like a white diamond
                         across the sky.
The godly animals, roused from sleep
—Flying serpents and the many-eyed of the ancients—
Come out to mate on the lawns of heaven
All about me a fierce fireworks of desire.

In such a moment I would make a necklace
Of these leaves, rustling and golden,
In vision of her the whirling winds have taken
Breathing into their sleeping veins
All power of earth air and fire
                 joyous in her love.
I would be no more sentient than this bird above me
Its breast against a receding wind
That is time broken by the beasts of heaven.

Ball

Where earth dropped into sun
   giant sky without stones
      I'm going—Mexico City to Veracruz
the road a great green fire

   I am smoked to dryness

Stars of smoke who made this road throw up
                              your eyes
    which are closed in New York

O weir I can not sing you from that quiet street
O prairies have not seen you close your eyes

A tomb of clouds to receive you
    by the fog in your veins
  BASHO
    eaten
by the sun from the page   I wait
                        as long
                      as a   star

[In a Grove]

```
                    o
              r         v
           g              e
         a                 h
              t         e
    n        i              l
I         w        I      e
     B         O    C    c        t
       o    V      E   t            h
    d    o               r            g
     o  m                 i         i
      w   i                c      n
       n   n                  y
                      g     b    b
                                   i
                                   r
                                   d
                                   s
                            I
                         put
                      my   ner
                    ves      over
                  my   eyes   my
                veins   over   my
              skin    and    think
           HA!       I     decipher
        the  talk   of   the  gods!
```

Resurrections

It is I who create the world and put it to rest
you will never understand me
I have willed your destruction

It's the beginning of the flower
inside its black ore I salute abyss after abyss

You are the exploding rose of my eyes I have nothing but third eyes

This is the end of clockwork sempiternity is the rose of time

This flower talk will get you nowhere

I will not be involved with people I call true distance
I invite you only to the door of horror
Laughter
I keep stoning you with black stars

        Christ is superior to Apollo
        bodhisattvas are drunk with being God
        he who is living lives only the living live
        I will hate and love in the Way
            in *this* is Being
I will return to the poem

        •

        A theater of masked actors in a trance
        according to the virtues of sacred plants

There are those dying of hunger
mankind is sanctioned crime
men should not die of hunger

There will come Judgment swift and terrible
war

my actor will say in mask of sick dying poor man
        I cast you into hell! I die to live
who will bring *you* back to life?

Against this another whirls in a frenzied controlled dance
he dreams on orgies dark forces revolve
demons
incinerations of the spirit
the Bomb
in its mushroom flower actions round a dumb Black Angel cloud

                •

I have never made a poem never emerged it's all a farce if I could
    unravel as this Raga into song
opulent view of Kashmir
thousands of images bearing light
light thru clouds the beauty of things
lit up slow unraveling of the morning

On a himalaya
this one in sight of heaven
outpouring
prayer of lungs sex eyes
eyes poured in abysms of light

the flight of horned heads
gods, cats, bulls, dogs, sphinxes
each head inside out a torso of fish

        Ranka uraniku
        bahaba hi olama
        sancu pantis droga
        harumi pahunaka

I never see enough
with those who fly tortoise shell in the infinite hangup
words slow unraveling song

the gods are vomiting
I am entering earth I am walled in light I am where the song is shot into my eyes *O hypodermic light!*

Hypodermic Light

It's absurd I can't bring my soul to the eye of odoriferous fire

my soul whose teeth never leave their cadavers
my soul twisted on rocks of mental freeways
my soul that hates music
I would rather not see the Rose in my thoughts take on
    illusionary prerogatives
it is enough to have eaten bourgeois testicles
it is enough that the masses are all sodomites
Good Morning
the ships are in I've brought the gold to burn Moctezuma
I'm in a tipi joking with seers I'm smoking yahnah
I'm in a joint smoking marijuana with a cat who looks like Jesus
    Christ
heroin is a door always opened by white women
my first act of treason was to be born!
I'm at war with the Zodiac
my suffering comes on as a fire going out O beautiful world
    contemplation!

It's a fact my soul is smoking!

•

That the total hatred wants to annihilate me!
it's the sickness of american pus against which I'm hallucinated
I'm sick of language
I want this wall I see under my eyes break up and shatter you
I'm talking all the poems after God
I want the table of visions to send me oriole opium
A state of siege
It's possible to live directly from elementals! hell stamps out
    vegetable spirits, zombies attack heaven! the marvelous put
    down by martial law, America fucked by a stick of marijuana
paper money larded for frying corpses!

Here comes the Gorgon! There's the outhouse!

Come up from dead things, anus of the sun!

•

old after midnight spasm
juke box waits for junk
round about midnight music
combing bop hair
getting ready to cook
Jupiter wails!
heroins of visionary wakeup in light of Bird and The Going Forth
    By Day
the pipe's spiritual brain winters off the Nile old hypodermic needle
    under foot of Anubis
                    Mother Death
I'm at the boat of Ra Set
I'm Osiris hunting stars his black tail of the sun
It's the end of melancholy   sad   bop   midnights.

•

They shot me full of holes at Kohlema's hut!
It's you who'll be butchered in my precise imagination
It'll be hard to withstand the reasoning of peyotl Rack

    many times my song went downstairs, people of entire hate and I
burned you in basements without tearing my face up
O people I hate the most! glass automobiles snake by to decay
    decay is living anthill
where yr automobiles lift their skirts and stiff
pricks of dead indians going in reverse
automobile graveyards where I eat fenders, bodies I crunch
    mustards of engines I devour whole gallons of molding chrome
    I whip cheese from cannibal hoods

O beautiful people of hate! your money fenders how creamy! your
    electric eyes stinking! your geometric reconstructions against
    my destructions!

•

U.S.S. San Francisco

No one completes a sentence I am in hell to complete it
above the cobalt bomb magic fog crawls in the hideous park of
   addicts
I buy ectoplasmic peanut butter
roaming streets empty of opium bridges open only to the south
Everyone has left
my compass points to the fifth direction in space your typewriter eyes
The beautiful Lul in a fog of peacocks
The beautiful Lul with swans in her face
The beautiful Lul turned into a statue floating the lake
The beautiful Lul who has taken my veins tied them to the bark
The beautiful Lul a vapor
her breasts vapor
her fingers vapor
her breasts vapor the beautiful Lul with lips
the beautiful lips of Lul phantom of the beautiful Lul
How ugly yr typewriter eyes not like the eyes of Lul gone a vapor
not like the last puff of opium gone a phantom vapor
O Lull I swim from albatross shark fins in game of light
O Lul your head gone to Egypt
O Lul your head city of Indian sand
O Lul
I stamp out roses of fire
O Lul
I drown in your eyes The anchor of heroin is thrown forever!

•

Immense blank void, melting structures, sperm steel, the last
   roasted cock, geometry of inert horizontal planes, phases of
   toxicomic monsters I open the door of the air!

My cock scratches the interior lint of fire, uncreated hair is the net
   thru which vaginal/anal spiders feel out corners of the universe
   —O cunt of bombs! true furniture for the Creator's habit-
   forming drugs.

An old man in a temple
shucking corn.

The Antiquities come out thru the curtain of Fuck, they have
　　reopened the holes of my arms
I keep chewing the leg of civilizations, at the origin of incest
　　morphine is equivalent to the apotheosis of cannibal
　　motherhood

Every time I smoke a cigarette the Creator has blinked all stars
　　time pebbles of water in a trillion second of man's sodomite
　　existence my words can not lie

It isn't a question of love it's how you find yourself out and that,
　　as the Master said, brings on anguish

"He who has known the world has found the body and he who
　　has found the body has known a corpse"

I see white alone from this horizontal plane of glass obscurity the
　　blackness I feed you is made to see white light

One day the quest for water was realized. I picked up arid cactus I
　　sucked out God and dreamt civilization. The quest for water
　　must go on!
　　　　　　　　　　　My friend keeps talking in my head of magic herb
Colombian Indians snort, shut their eyes seeing clouds and float
around like clouds
I'm looking for the seeds of the Virgin.

•

In camera of sempiternity you walk around figures molding dust

Amapola in white light Amapola before tribunes of furniture
　　history
Amapola of Tepic in dreams of sand shore where spectral image of
　　my friend John
Amapola of sempiternal Orient
black star of Amapola

49

white look of Amapola from a mountain of walls
Amapola commands night
seers shift in stars Amapola in clutches of white lice
escape of Amapola thru pyramids of lost light alone Amapola alone
flight of Corby night
Amapola in a forest of persian tapestries
Amapola the taste of spiritual sugar
                         Amapola in gardens of Araby
               Amapola born east   murdered in the west

Fin del Mundo

The poem says the bombs of America went off—mothers rotting
   that the chicks of war hatch and scream ANATHEMA!

The poem says you only think you're alive but about to be born
   your radioactive heliographs mock the moon's tongue.

Death is around the corner waving decrepit hands at the poem
   saying "what begins as a transparent globe turns into an
   abstract skull"

What wave mantic eye what wave cutting chairs of my soul what
   wave claws forth psychopathic night and vomits lungs and keys
   wave sucking silent wave thru demented cities.

The poem says JUNK IS KING movieflashback to antique loveroom
   ossified sex organ room in the poem's mouth saying
at whorehouse in tropics Ananka high priestess of a secret cult
at Miramol thru jungles of copper bells—

I wake up in vapors antediluvian climates circle my room I'm
   twisted in a sea of motion I break out forms of antique script
   20 leaves fall in leaden blights OH MUDDIED MIRES OF MY TIME!

Destroyed works walk out of walls into me into the poem saying it
   is an ogre's hand rocks my living tables it is a vast cloth
   of cotton folds my body it is heart of sleep I live Visage
   in atomic night of dark triumph where walls of the poem are
   fixed in fire at the flying dragon's emanation thruout space.

Within me is the power to BE! TO LIVE! The dead are dead and the
   living—live!

•

        At the sleeper of inveterate cars
Behemoth at entrance to the labyrinth
        I take the image of the letter 10

Over infinite carpet rolled sideways
                  I am hidden by funnels of feather
Who looks in stone changes mirrors into boats canals into weathers
                  and the masters of pestilence draw up
                  clock doom's head
wasted waters
                  opulent neck of the Indiana monster
shrieking with voices of terrorized women and children!

                  I make the gesture
A domed sky of flying tombs converges
                  Queen of sand King in the mountain's mouth
HEAR THE MONSTER BUGGER THE MONSTER CRAZE THE MONSTER
    COME OUT!

                  I think a star in monster's mouth
Incisions of frosted flowers take up on its lake
                  its clouds turn into iron hooks
its oceanic tower turns in yr entrails

                  My breath is bridge into the Monster's
mechanics it is fear — Ocean — ocean of its roaring cry bring down
magic
        horse rhythms in flight opening
                  gone into the Monster's sound!

The Wheel

       At halls of Oedipus blind
           at interior cairn at Carnac
               at jaguar court of the Quiché flue
I came with Saint-Germain
  washed the feet of lepers dried the tears of widows
    walked a long way to the desert meditated birds
      went the way of wandering anchorite
        chewed the bread of hawks
          looped the dream of Constantine
            was Bishop of Alchemia
              made signs for the people that they knew the Christ
             opened gates of Saint Bruno
            sat still in cave of Saint Druida
          spoke out against the rule of iron.

I came with banquet of lovers at ruins of Tenochtitlan
  swam the Hellespont of antique mystery
    landed on shores of Mu Atlantis Babylon
      made fast for pool of the underworld and
        ascended feet high into the sky—at rigalu of Tingis
      ate from tables of undersea gardens.

I came in company of the unknown saint
  prayed to Nôtre Dame in women's cabinets
    entered hermitages of Basil talked desert tongues
      was desperate in the medieval night
        designed crests for the Duc d'Ys
          brought battle on the anglosaxon world.

      Soul in the night
    make the wearer rise with Thee
  to drink with Thee the wines of paradise.
I came with Thee, anointed One, into mechano hells at
  desecrations of the Lily and said
No more this door/ for Love turns in happy feet of fat light we
  watch with eagle eyes
in time and out of time—for Thee.

Deamin

What are you watching I am watching that we are watching
I watch the heads, they watch me
automobiles watch me I don't watch them
make underpasses overpasses—but pass me by!

Watching watching watching watching watching!
There *is* some way out of Guerrero Street! there must be!
when will he come with the big hypo?

It's what's watching me from the spoon
it's what's watching me turn on
it's what's going on inside the ampule

                Boats at Veracruz place to score a plane to Beirut

it's all over watching arabs cop for coffee and tea
    that must be the way!

                poets are outlawed the army has been digested by
heroin the white house evaporated the morphine president's shade
is flapping the asses of Dar beginning of which/maelstroms of
Poe and apache ghost
           f l a m i n g   across!
what a mess! a scene out of time capsule last days of the world

You must imagine coming of Inca prince
my dim scopolomine feather universe from back of my head

This much is certain: the gathering of opium's a delicate art
the rocks of America are not beautiful
the dark oil genii has grown into a monster
           claw of the Mummy out of the wheatfield

There is no agrarian program it is all economic war!
I make war! I decide this tribe, cool! this nation, spared!
    this stupidity unlimited, putdown! this slumbering beauty,
                                  waked up!
        this heap, fuckup, dead bitch—run down, put
                                  down, finished!

        I liquidate by magic!

From the Front

Tenochtitlan!
grey seven thousand feet high
mist of dust — tin door open
to slow motion immobilized traffic
— girl at window — terrace —
terrace a heartmobile —
wind! dust of wind — wind!

sail of dead ghost opium people
fantast — the fields of Egluria

these watches promote me
venetian blinds, Chicagos of Zeno

The mountain erupts
land masses grab the Pacific
earthquakes
the sky is peeling its skin off!

Is this American mood? 1960 weather beasts,
    who tampers the moon tides?

Reprieve. Sail of dust wind
venetian mountain sequence
zeroguns silence the street
mute traffics — desperate surrealism
backfire from motorcycles
waves over empty rooftops

Geneva of movies, who ate the dogbrick sandwich?
I've cut a loaf of it
and splattered eiou — chaos
slamming venetian blinds
click, the cat asleep
      aloha, tidal waves

Where am I? you answer
the question where am I?
who's here? who wants Veracruz?
what is New York? who is San Francisco?
Friend
where are you?
what to do   go where   how?

Motorcycles of atonal venetian blind dust of wind rooftop!

Still Poems

Vacuous suburbs

This silence doors shut against animals, spirits,
naked women over rooftops tearing down twenty pieces of ham
this will never be admitted to public record
policemen imbedded under phantom rails

      Can you find the dinosaur's track?
      Can you put yr hands on telephone wires?
      Can you find Socrates in some garden?

Red Indian spirits come thru veils of blood tears torment
These hours are still not put to rest
arrows mark the dawn!
gloom bell breaks
They shall not peer from windows
their souls shut up outside fungus tree
holding back spiritual floodgates
eyes don't catch ghost fires the spirits have deserted them
they who set up bad vibrations people more ghostly than dead
    Indians—
sleeping in bed knots of nothing.

•

This is the grey limit
suddenly a great voice booms no one hears it
a car goes by
typewriter keys have meaning my fingers have meaning my pains
    at back of head have meaning
there's a slight breeze I can tell because the curtains are moving as if
in a dream sequence

It's a drab world just a few sounds indifference
I'm happy now thinking on love way beyond contraries dullness
    zero hours

It's the way it is and I'm a god!

•

There's a mountain of houses upside down it's dawn nothing really
    matters much
you'll never be rich — I accept! this is love I'm going to love
    because I'm already there
This is my mind talking
NOT ideas machines — anyone else's opinion
what's important is not seen by eyes nor heard by ears
what goes on behind appearances
Pax! it's here! I know it at last!
Someone some one else some vortex of meeting final crystal open
    crystal beautiful crystal
nothing else matters
I'm falling from high places
It's so beautiful there are no images anymore
there IS a presence there IS a light there IS
    this incomprehensible transparent land
        sudden/complete.

•

The night is a space of white marble
This is Mexico
I'm sitting here, slanted light fixture, pot, altitudinous silence
your voice, Dionysius, telling of darkness, superessential light
In the silence of holy darkness I'm eating a tomato
I'm weak from the altitude
something made my clogged head move!
Rutman a week at beach at Acapulco
Carol Francesca waiting till Christmas heroin rain on them!
I see New York upside down
your head, Charlie Chaplin — in a sling
it's all in the courts of war
                sign here — the slip of dung
technically we are all dead
this is my own thought! a hail of hell!
Saint Dionysius reminds us of flight to unknowable Knowledge
the doctrine of initiates completes the meditation!

•

There is this distance between me and what I see
everywhere immanence of the presence of God
no more ekstasis
a cool head
watch watch watch
I'm here
He's over there . . . It's an Ocean . . .
sometimes I can't think of it, I fail, fall
There IS this look of love
there IS the tower of David
there IS the throne of Wisdom
there IS this silent look of love
Constant flight in air of the Holy Ghost
I long for the luminous darkness of God
I long for the superessential light of this darkness
another darkness I long for the end of longing
I long for the
          it is Nameless what I long for
a spoken word caught in its own meat saying nothing
This nothing ravishes beyond ravishing
There IS this look of love Throne Silent look of love

•

I have given fair warning
Chicago New York Los Angeles have gone down
I have gone to Swan City where the ghost of Maldoror may still
   roam
The south is very civilized
I have eaten rhinoceros tail
It is the last night among crocodiles
Albion opens his fist in a palm grove
I shall watch speckled jewel grow on the back of warspilt horses
Exultation rides by
A poppy size of the sun in my skull
I have given fair warning
at the time of corpses and clouds I can make love here as
   anywhere.

Morning Light Song

RED DAWN clouds coming up! the heavens proclaim you, Absolute
    God
I claim the glory, in you, of singing to you this morning
For I am coming out of myself and Go to you, Lord of the
    Morning Light
For what's a singer worth if he can't talk to you, My God of Light?
These lines should grow like trees to tie around yr Crown
    of the Sky
These words should be strong like those of the ancient makers,
                        O poet of poets
           Ancient deity of the poem —
Here's spindle tongue of morning riding the flushes of NIGHT
Here's gigantic ode of the sky about to turn on the fruits of my lyre
Here's Welcome Cry from heart of the womb of words, — Hail,
    Queen of Night!
Who giveth birth to the Morning Star, Here's the quiet cry of
    stars broken among crockery
Here's the spoon of sudden birds wheeling the rains of Zeus
Here's the worshipping Eye of my soul stinging the heavens
Here's Charmed Bird, zepher of High Crags — jugs of the divine
    poem
As it weaves terrestial spaces, overturning tombs, breaking hymens
From where cometh this first cry
                that my hands go into for the wresting of words
Here's my chant to you, Morning of mornings, God of gods, Light
    of light
Here's your singer let loose into the sky of your heaven
For we have come howling and screaming and wailing and I come
    SINGING
To You who giveth forth the song of songs that I am reborn from
    its opulence
That I hold converse with your fantasy That I am your beauty
NOT OF THIS WORLD and bring to nothing all that would stop me
    from flying straight to your heart whose rays conduct me to
    the SONG!

High

O beato solitudo! where have I flown to?
stars overturn the wall of my music
as flight of birds, they go by, the spirits
opened below the lark of plenty
ovens of neant overflow the docks at Veracruz
This much is time
summer coils the soft suck of night
lone unseen eagles crash thru mud
I am worn like an old sack by the celestial bum
I'm dropping my eyes where all the trees turn on fire!
I'm mad to go to you, Solitude—who will carry me there?
I'm wedged in this collision of planets/Tough!
I'm ONGED!
I'm the trumpet of King David
the sinister elevator tore itself limb by limb

        You can not close
        you can not open
        you break yr head
        you make bloody bread!

Jeanlu

By the window cut in half Jeanlu
Jeanlu in the opulent night her breast riding the sky
Jeanlu asleep like a nautilus smiling at Victor Hugo
Jeanlu bared on the branches coming from my third eye
Jeanlu if it is a candle of fire women blue in the night Jeanlu!
Where the borders break the caskets of lovers — MASK! — Jeanlu
In spite of icicles fed from flamingos Jeanlu
whenever wandering fauns drown and are reborn Jeanlu
going down in a dream of descending demolitions Jeanlu
waiting! waiting! as sponges of the sea in love Jeanlu
The earth is emptying Jeanlu
                soon spansules of eternity
           explode you Jeanlu
      Jeanlu who is
           seer sperm.

Infernal Muses

Go! my calf-headed drone! O sheep-faced Ana Stekel
turning into dove's dung, Ana Black Ana Noir
over niagra of bureau lips, rococo of bad taste
your brassier window of New York drenched in marijuana rain
Bianca dead on the chessboard field
Bianca of torn-down elevators Bianca projected from mexican days
    of the dead
in true baroque dream
at the house in shape of a monstrance
only there on rotten colonial street autos de fe for you, Bianca
    jet song of blood fires in yr toenails walls of yr great cunt
    emblazoned in bile!
I'm choking to see you Bianca
Bianca a vapor
at blackfender stockings burning witches hair
at obelisk of crayfish mornings mysterious Daughter Scorpiana
who nailed the corpse of wood on flesh
Scorpiana sculpted in white opium
head of Scorpiana circled by entrails
Scorpiana flown from wounds of women beaten to death by the
    Gestapo

Ana Black   Ana Noir   Ana Stekel   Bianca   Scorpiana
    Scorpiana   Bianca   Ana Noir   Ana Black   Ana Stekel

Subconscious Mexico City New York

How depressing here I am after my nerves tonged hell!
cut in two by flames
not caring who you are my friend my enemy one inside the other
I am always walking in pain
Somnambulists in green shoes are hung on ladders over street's
    mirage
they disappear in artificial fogs transformed into lupines
I am out in the day dying in it
I am thrown as a cluster of old sounds into the park
Blacksuited men having no faces stare into statues I WANT THEM
    TO WALK!
from frozen eyes the ray shall dart to finish off the population!
BLACK BLOOD RUNS FROM GREY STATUES
the unbreakable record turns in my skull
I have put a lemon tree in my window over the sphinx in my
    window I have put a veil
it is possible that no one exists
I am turned out of sadistic breasts turned into statuary it's the
    lemon tree burning in my window
all this time I am sick
my nerve ends fart
I dream of shit
maledictions press my hand in public places
I have thrown away a foot-long hypodermic needle into Central Park

•

Parades melt eternally where the park turned itself inside out
cups of ballerina mint tea float the vaginal shopwindows
that I am tortured in museums of frozen fifth avenue crowd
the sun is eclipsed by junk eyes
all that liquid money! in yr mouth, Maggie!
cocktails, rackety rack, cocktails — blonde jazz hair
I'm whirling back by furious subway
            lion on the platform / coffee sand and cubalibres
winter's blue tooth ravaging lonely Flamingo on the Hudson

I'm the solar dictator blown away fragments down floating
   woman's water

down the streets by snowbird

·

I cut out, I mean there was no proper head to the time
inside it by gilted raindrop of telephone
to no room—just floor—
I cut out
that is, flight into ancient gods, birds and men shaped as tunnels
   of solar stone
going back over old road plastered down by sky

CACTUS
inhalations of Tloloc expansive drives of rain
now, head of five flowing fingers
the bush of fire behind old cobblestone canon
Quetzalcoatl's passage from the moon to the sun
at heart of the process, spiritual war to pyramidic contemplation
the Toltecs set up 500 B.C., even to Moctezuma's time

    burning water ran thru Chapultepec

       cut out to old Tollan.

Rompi

—Rompi! Tangier! Rompi!

I fell into night the genii came
terrible genii nailing me into a coffin
This witness between you and the prophet of my dreams
I almost died in dream of death
the genii were cruel
kif/kif the genii were cool
      they let me live

From cape of no highs
to somaliland of antique drums
—ganja in the veldt—
swimming fish fly far to far-flung regions
—Africa in my head
leopards of light
tigers of tons of terror
devil masks coming out of every tree!
—watching warriors of the watusi way, I wail with thee!

O gingers of arabic gum!
O sweet kiss of the melon!

Where do they hang from, the ouds of King David?
Songs of oriental america
ring from rafters of my heart
kif/kif—*swing!* rock and roll arab

      all this way to Allah the merciful

Blue Grace

            crashes thru air
where Lady LSD hangs up all the floors of life for the last time
Blue Grace leans on white slime
Blue Grace weaves in & out of Lüneburg and "My Burial Vault"
    undulates
from first hour peyote turn on
Diderot hand in hand with the Marquis de Sade
wraps himself up in a mexican serape
at Constitution Hall, Philadelphia, 1930

Blue Grace turns into the Count of Saint-Germain
      who lives forever
           cutting up George Washington
dream of pyramid liquefactions from thighs of Versailles

Blue Grace intimidates Neville Chamberlain
feels up Filippo Marinetti
and other hysterics of the phallic rose

Blue Grace dressed up as automobile sperm
    My Claw of the future
    and the almond rose Rich the Vampire wears
               over the US Army
—FLAGS!
      AMERICAN FLAGS!
            flying like bats
          out of "My Burial Vault!"
flood museums
         where Robespierre's murder is plotted
              —floated from Texcoco,
the Prince of Bogota caught red-handed
sniffing forty cans of Berlin ether!

             Heydrich ice-blue teeth
      impersonates, psychokinetically,

the resurrection of Blue Grace as prophetess of the anti-planet
   system

Blue Grace under dark glasses
getting out of one hundred white cars at once!
Cars of ectoplasmic tintypes
go to the juncture where Blue Grace Glass is raped
        at the Court of Miracles, Mexico City, 1959

Blue Grace undressed
reveals tattoo marks of Hamburg, sea & storm of
                Neptune-Pluto conjunction
Rumors of war
strafe the automation monster
walking to universal assassination
K & K and the russian poets
suck Blue Grace's opulent morsels, back & front
The nicotine heaven of Bosch's painting
emanates the thousand beauties of
      Christopher Maclaine's tool box
of mechanical brass jewels
                Man,
                the marvel
                of masturbation arts,
            intersects Blue Grace
   at World's Finale Orgasm Electro-Physic Apocalypse!

I sing the beauty of bodily touch
with my muse, Blue Grace

The Ancients Have Returned Among Us

in a way humming thru crystals of light — most unexpected —
      the ancients sizzle and dazzle
  not as we imagined nor can put our machines to nor
      make comprehensible by words or songs or metaphors
      The ancients have truly returned to us
      and have unfurled flags of sudden Cloud Rings
    from rivers crossing the most ordinary streets
   on the way back from mediterranean flowers whose lips
  sip the leaf-elevators of the natural man buried in the
dreams whose chrysalis snaps from the Dragon
     of fortuitous events whispered at the Age of Cham
& sent hurtling from the steeples of Og
    I can hear the ancients from the mouth of
fog &   dazzling wind sonatas beloved of hunchback adepts
& dismembered mummies whose Living Light
  crackles from the diapason of This Constant Present Moment
   they use as a bridge to remind me to be silent
   & seal my words by carbon honeys & not to spare
   the endless rolls of cellophane reaching Saturn
   by the cross-fibred necropolis of the Hanged Man:
they caution me to Flamboyant Order
  that repeats the dooms ordained by the transfiguration
   of the banners of wayward heralds whose brains
     fall blandly & sedately & fall again
  through the overdrenched factories of neon blindness
   & who cares? since it is all known to have been
  fixed in the calendars of the Twins & read
       throughout prehistory from the Secret Stones
cast on the Shadow: The ancients have returned
  & unfurl repeatedly into your Ear the scroll
  of living legends, the talk of multiplying flowers
foamed over books without words in libraries
     built by fire to the laboratory that dissolves
    constantly into an ocean of antimatter
    Truly the wisdom of the ancients is written everywhere you can

                    not see it and
        secreted nowhere other than through the tachygraph
                under the cascade of capillary mountains
            forever registered before this instant gave birth to
        its opposite which is snaking beyond the distance
                    between you and me moonman & opal of the sun
            This arrangement by special decree of what
                turns night into day or brings the longest night
before the Lion that rips open the throat of the New Year
                when the ancients were the youngest gods burst
                from the bubbles of sperm spit   Listen!
        their music played from buzz & bleats
                you can not hear except through periscopes
                    set down among vascular whales
            mating from the crisis of rock & shale under
                the disappearing atlantis of corn cultures &
        reappearing before the wheat altars on
                    the plains of the western wind & western winter from
                which the words & letters were handed down
                the elevators of Tomorrow over the Deluge
            the great night giant sends us today by blood-lined
        cups swollen with ichor & flames throbbed from
                        lyres lost to
                    Sothis & returning from under that Sea
    whose waves break from the Iris of the Ibis:
                    These cups that flow like banners of molten lead
                Cups put together by Tartesian Giants
                hallucinated by the saints of Ys
                unveiled in allegories of the Tower floating the
                hearts of children
        cups whose brims overcrowd the rustling autumn
                    Door to the invisible temple built unseen
            in cities of the satanic machine
                    Cups the legends reveal and the ancients
                are beginning to pass around as it they were ordinary
            milk bottles for the children newly born from
                    top branches of the Tree with its roots
                        going back
                        to the starfields of Every Night.

71

She Speaks the Morning's Filigree

> *Beneath him, earth's breath*
> *risen from inward wars of blood:*
> *youth's vision*
> *is a vibrant string plucked by the gods*
> *over the field of stars*

Through the night on fire with my blood
whose incense sputters your sleep and washes you
on the threshold caught from the Tinging Stone
I'm tired of cooking the ultimate specter of future poems
weak from demands of the mooneating children of the 25th century
it's really so late to proclaim my youth of a hundred years

But you, Io,
walking on sandals of almond & wrapped by hair of eglantine,
open the seashell that sings us back through storms of smoke
to the burnt altars of childhood that float
in milk I drew from dragons slain with the help of the sylph:
Clocks rant their dirges of woe to no avail.

Your sleep is my awakening
All the shadows lie canceled by celestial foam
Moon-poisons are cooked to the perfection of Tea
The sun stirs the cauldron Sothis fixes from your tears
that dance as diamonds on opalescent hands breaking the Seven
    Seals!
Over & over the dusk of the Chant from the plain of Segovia
rings up the veil through which the deities move prisms of desire:
the cup that swallows the sword, the wands that shake the stars.

Aurora the cat of the morning
has sent a message of aerial fire
to the twelve-faced Aerolith whose name is not permitted for
    reading
whose number is water & abyss of the bone
whose age is always about to become and
has always been no less than time

We can play host to the marvelous
and have it burn us to the salt of memory
where an invisible stone contracts all thought
to draw out the words
that shall crackle your sleep
to wake us up beyond the Pleiades

No longer tired now I've supt from the tombs of kings
and raced past the Giant Chairs of Tartesos
to mark the spectrum's path to where you and I
shall be buried in the seed of the Sun
I'm at the gate of the house built by no one
but the One who pulled it down
before it was founded from the sperm of the walking sleeper!
From this place my poems can begin
to take on the shape of candles
        and incense sticks

       as you ride midnight mares
       to undo the astral curse
            turn pages of burning books
                        or float
           freely
    on the morning's filigree.

Voice of Earth Mediums

We are truly fed up
with mental machines of peace & war
nuclear monoxide brains, cancerous computers
motors sucking our hearts of blood
that once sang the choruses of natural birds
We've had enough dynamos & derricks
thud-thud-thudding valves & pulleys
of the Devil Mankin's invention
          And soon
if they aren't *silenced*
and we survive the sacrificial altars
of the automobile god and the vulvas of steel
spitting molecular madness
through layers of satanic dust

if the complete crowd-manacled Machine
isn't *dissolved, back into the Earth*
from where its elements were stolen
          we shall call on
the Great Ocean Wave
Neter of waters
and the King of Atlantis & his snake spirits
otherwise known as
          Orcus
          Dagon & Drack
to send up calamitous tidal waves
—a thousand feet high, if need be—
to bury all the monster metal cities
and their billion, bullioned wheels of chemical death
Oh, William Blake
thou can overseer, if it please thee,
this lesson of Aquarius Clean Sweep
that Earth's beautiful spirit of purifying Ocean
shall stop these weights on and plunder of
her metal blood and very thin skin
to teach us Terra's song of taoist harmonies

What Is Not Strange?

Sea towers of Sicily
  change place with the tongues
    of elephants borne on the back
      of the Ibis
        What is *not* strange
          among eddies of the
            hermaphrodite
              caught on the spiked hair
                of foam—your lips, Diotima
                result from the broken statues
            of Hermes & open
          with the click
          of all the fans of Murasaki
        What is not strange is
  that
the shorelines of zipzap cities
explode giant coke bottles
  lighting the savage factories
    supercharging
      morning blur to
        Venus—Ping!
          Visionary hot rodders
            tear off their clothes before you, Geronimo:
            Epiphany
              in a star-spangled leather jacket
                flapping on the hammocks
                  of the bivouac girls
                    back from their raids on the moon.
              What is *not* strange
                opening up sassafras seeds,
              golden whistles and millenniums
            of Pest at a single glance from Superman
            —he who is not coming back ever—
          as the Holy Biscuits

      spill endlessly dollar bills the future
    shall print their poems on!
What is not strange?
now that I've swallowed the Pacific Ocean
    and sabotaged the Roman Empire
      and you have returned
        from all your past lives
          to sip the snakes of my fingertips:

    Go Away & Be Born No More

    Do a Kundalini Somersault

Astro-Mancy

The stars have gone crazy
and the moon is very angry
The old civilization
that rolled the dice of Hitler
is surely bumbling
into a heap of catatonic hysteria
Another civilization
secret for six thousand years
is creeping on the crest of
future, I can almost see the
tip of its triangular star
I'm writing this from lost Atlantis
I wonder when I'll get back
to the alchemical castle
where I can rebegin my work
left off in the Middle Ages
when the Black Beast roared down
on my weedy parchments and spilled me
into an astral waiting room
whose angels, naturally in flaming white robes,
evicted me for this present irony:
idleness, mancy & the Dream
instead of getting down to
the super-real work of
transmuting the Earth *with love of it*
by the Fire prepared from the time of On!
No matter, I'm recovering
from a decade of poisons
I renounce all narcotic
& pharmacopoeic disciplines
as too heavy 9-to-5-type sorrows
Instead I see America
as one vast palinode
that reverses itself completely until

Gitchi Manito actually returns
as prophet of a new Iroquois Brotherhood—
this needs further development—
I foresee a couple of
essential changes:
a Break Out Generation
of poet-kings setting up
The Realm Apart
of sweet natural play
and light metal work
matter lovingly heightened
by meditation, and spirit
transmuted into matter,
the whole commune conducted by
direct rapid transcription
from a no-past reference
antirational, fantastically poetic
violently passive and
romantically unprejudiced
Each one his own poet
and poetry the central fact
food & excrement of culture
I see you smiling tolerantly
O liberal lip (another utopian
bites the dust) but no! you just
can't see what I'm reading while
in the act of transcribing it
I know at least three other
supernatural souls who envision
much the same under different names,
but the nomenclature's not more than
the lucid panorama I telescope
as, on this summer night's
torpor, it passes from under my eyelid and

grabs you, earth returned,
into the middle of Aquarius, one millennium forward.

Coat of Arms

Pure as gale and mist washing my skull
pure as silk dances on the ocean's knee
    thong thighs of the walking coast
pure as Mendocino witch havens
    through the transparent plumes of extinct birds
looking down from the sky-people boat
exploding over candy castles
    the salt wisdom pervades
safe as the mummy's purity *is* from the congresses of fear

The night goes up
into the ventricles of King Novalis
and horned men descend the saline stairway
whose bones are lit up from astral lamps
of the great genii, Ignis phana, pure claw
that brushes death's meat
awakened without a body on the edge of the club-footed wave

Going around blind corners, the sylph
breaks her teeth on the borders of three continents
I pass without passports—
rapid vision overtakes the storm
of this glittering void I love
and reveals everything in a speeding cloud

This is the moral for inventing ecstasies
Freed from the clutch of memory
I eat the eagle's windy branches
    my eye the lion's cave
silver fluids fix my voice
that sings *The World and I Are One*
What's newly hatched is born from dying seed

To let loose a room's inner skeleton
I come from far places
dressed in the explosions of green lamps

It's the moment before arson
Taught not to look back
my fires drink a porous stone
    The geyser speaks
    at the house of the onyx mirror
    My name is augur
    these lips besmirch the dawn
    My sword's a vaporous cloud
The tooth marks of ecstasy
wear the look of totems
and the dragon's vermouth tongue
Every arm is bathed in silver blood
    I read the spells of Egypt patiently

Even if I could not reach you, *supreme opal,*
the carnivorous sea is avenged
even if you erased the cornerstone of the temple
against the door melting with pride
I would marry all the stars sitting on the face of the sea
like a traditional wolf of the absolute
sucking down the dish served up by the flood

O ponder the gaze of the forest
Raise mist from the shore
There's this gull punished by clouds
on the inevitable hour of genetic infantries
and a war on oracles
After history has washed her head
the grail heroes move over gigantic chess sets

Am I passive enough yet
to breathe the fire of the opal?
And walk over my graves
that withstood the cleavages of insect wars?
To wake up from death, *satisfied*

    the forest before me
replaced
        by a cartilage of stars

Blue Locus

It's here the glove attacks the hand
Everything is splendidly distant
your torso carved out of daylight
on the screaming horizon I've ceased to hear
because you secrete a whisper and the clouds tremble

The squirrel you feed is the familiar of halos
trailing your thoughts from the spirit lake
blue locus
promising the unknown on a hike to the woods

There must be a playroom of totems
under the lake you raise with the key by which you read my lips
On the fur road you travel
I'm to steal the squirrel's eye
. . .which is how the sun looks when asleep . . .
and nail it over the photoglyph
in the space where you've cropped your head off

I want to play fanatically over your daylight
see the thunder-bridge return to the font
and bring you to where the dream emanates
through the paper-shackling reality
full optics
drenched with the juice of chance

O my lady of combustible cameo
your mouth of the northern lights
doubt's ease
and our blistering profanations
no more answers
you are writing the poem
who burn me with your shadow
that your body veils wet arrows
the birds that circle you
        breastplates
  for the army of love

The Talisman

Only for those who love is dawn visible throughout the day
and kicks over the halo at the pit of ocean
the diamond whirls
all that's fixed is volatile
and the crushed remnants of sparrows travel without moving

I find myself smoking the dust of myself
hurled to the twilight
where we were born from the womb of invisible children
so that even the liver of cities
can be turned into my amulet of laughing bile

Melted by shadows of love
I constellate love with teeth of fire
until any arrangement the world presents
to the eyes at the tip of my tongue
becomes the perfect food of constant hunger

Today the moon was visible at dawn
to reflect o woman the other half of me you are
conic your breasts gems of the air
triangle your thighs delicate leopards in the wood where
   you wait

Luminous

I touch you with my eyes when you lie under spiders of silk
I touch you with my one-hundred-headed giraffes too secret to
    be seen
the rods & cones the morning covets awaken you
with my touch of tobacco eyes
and you rise from the snail's bed of tubular hair
I touch you with the breath of jet planes
and they are gone elsewhere to touch you too
I won't have you touched by sordid saints
I touch you with the hour that drips scent
snared from the chain of immaculate lice
who avenge themselves forever on the holy of holies
I touch you with the wind heaving the breasts of the morning
I touch you in the overcrowds
and they vanish
replaced by all the women who resemble you
and I touch them with the eyes of the sun

Annihilation of priests
I touch you on the threshold of the totem
carbon salt on the breath of the world
I touch you with my intricate rose superior to the fog
I touch you with heartstrings of the veiled mountain
whose magnetic moment is the sight of us making love
I rend your skirt by the wind stolen from ancient castles
your legs secrete the essence of wheat
and your ankles brush the wing of crow
Your lips touch alchemic gold torn from the femur bone of poetry
whispering through archives of your smile
that beguiles the oracle who has a headache to change his legends
I touch your earlobe with the fatal elegance of the peacock lip
your convulsions gallop my heart of the rose hermetic and flushed
    by goats sighting prey
I touch your nipples

that touch heaven that is all of you touching me
the temple of your hips
the morning glory of your sex
the miracle of bedsheets and the sacrament of sweat

Rhythms of your thighs are the music of the spheres
and all light has been given to veil you from the murderers of love

I touch your presence undressing the furniture
whose cries fill the distance between us
and you shall hear
when I touch you with telepathic tendrils
for then I'll come into you the light of the waking dream

Ephemeris

The room has lips to speak antediluvian wishes
        cloud wing of forest
                carbonic eye from the sea
The child has lost his way and found
His human breakfast table fast by the coral shore
Morning scales the mountain
With the palpitating flower I found in my mailbox
        unknown hydra service
            aerolith express

The conjurations at noon on the streets of the most industrious cities
For the advent of purple arachnids
For a rain of butterflies
The simultaneous apparition of flame-lined ladies from the cedar beds of the future

      X Magician
             at once to seed the air
                  with musk giants
Clouds grow so softly under your skirts
I can watch the children climbing the diamond temples at every corner
And there's a taste of bituminous wine
For the solar incubation so rarely conjured
But for your hair shedding the stars
        O little girls of the forest of cities

Out of My Hat of Shoals

Out of my hat of shoals
Mixed ladies in a park of seals
Transvestite fire and wink of water
Green flame rapes the garden tulips
Trees of nonsense bend their songs
Lips of clouds and kites of pain
I'm at a shower of windows
All the houses are made of rain
No more speed   we float
I'm happy with hermetic games
The toys of sleeping mathematicians
Triangles and compass of water
Theorems beyond reason
Hypnotic ladies read the future with the sweat of roses
I comb the stars
And they undress the moon with their nipples
The hunt is on
No one will ever sleep again
Sweet music of epicene bodies
All is pregnant with mystery
And the idols have been eaten up
Marigolds fume in the night
The day is locked in a box at sea
The sun has finally married the moon

The Analog

And the sea moved over the terrace into my marble stomach
that I saw the cleft on the rock disclose the Mason's Word
upon which were built the crumbling remains of On
treasure shored up from my inner eyes
the victuals medieval cathedrals secrete secretly
for the likes of the adepts
who smile through the velvet fissures of the centuries
that are Waves & Blankets of Stars
under which we are given, if we burrow long enough
for the hidden script, the Key to the King's Shut Chamber
that vanishes into the night hot with luminations
re-seered at the ice trance permitted to the high flyers
who with the correct gesture
at the right time know the precise moment
the Zodiac favors the conflagration of water and
the stillness of things about to become
when fire reabsorbs its opposite
the snarling snake before the plumage of the perfectly secured
    Peacock
Perchance the wave falls prematurely and spoils the little work
the Operator must beforehand arm himself with traditional shields
so that translated into the occult veins of his visible anatomy
the fox & falcon hoods spill volumes and sweat beacons
to throw him into the path which has no way up or down
and is never either way to the Ravaging Ferocious Mountain
    . . . Ah what am I saying that my lips might be burned by angels
    and sirens?

Fantast

From a jet plane window I landed into an eighteenth-century drawing room
Where the Marquis de Sade and I were of one mind tasting pineapples
Cameo brooches burst and showered us with pomegranate fumes
From the wrists of Doctor Mesmer little commercial empires sprouted sent on slow boats to Boston Harbor
Where I'm smoking Copley Square by the laughing wheels of the trains of totemic beasts
Spirit-lined
I proclaim the empire of molten man one with all his precious stones
The trees of America light up the specters of Cotton Mather
Happily we shall live my hair burning the snow
My eyes burning forever over the Rockies Hello Chief Seattle

Horse Angel

This word or this image
Whether the immense void to be filled from the ancients to now
Or the nightmare mane staring with crazy hypnotic starving eyes
Out of the oft-seen painting of Blake's friend Fuseli
Don't know
But am tied to a thousand grecian pillars their horse nostrils
   migrating
And the stillness does not inflict any ice on their great hairs

     An upside-down Golden Fleece

The horse pervades
Horses superior to machines
Horses lighted with blue oil flame from the factories

Horses watch me from my travels and metamorphose into mules
Transmigrating continents
     The donkey at Tangier
     And his burro on the road to Tamazunchale
     The road mendicant who was a giant of solar light Blind
        Indian
     And the moorish woman with the campesino straw hat
        sitting on a bag of esparto grass
All horse cultures
And the horse in dreams!
If I could speak of their manes hanging like metals
Hoofs tapping the rocks
And that wild look straight ahead in a fertile valley
                                  the sun

Flaming Teeth

The earthquake slivers
The broken nails of the nazis
Mister Fly and his obsidian mask
My father on his razor
Basalt nightmares
Megalithic godplanes click the xylophones
My wracking spit spits
Words are magic beans
Children of the flat-faced musicians
Cross the street into subtropical ice
Manuring down your hand split a hundred ways
By the onyx of baptism
Stop
I'm climbing
To genocide the look of you
A thousand shacks
human faces
Synthetic clouds
O for the slaughter America pinned on its bottom
I'd give up the rasp of Europe
Beatific visions sprawled on coat hangers
And weigh the silence with real screws
The fists of dawn
I'm still too intelligent
Become waste of years
Cruel whistling from under the snow inside the floorboards
And asleep drugged poet
You're safe striking the buttocks of the dream machine

Endless
Filth
Phanes

With the 24 electromagnetic

With rich tongue doorway briar and the lost look of Astatara
With bleeding pens
Dracula coins are the final exchange
"M" on all the rooftops signs the invisible with your blood
    imperial
And no more tempests in the tombs
Put them to sleep with the war angels
Which are all the angels

•

I'm a monster in my work plates
Over glades of dark statues that churn your retina priests of the
    Drag
And the dust I clean my sugar with
Knock down smoke over the everglades I'm american as rusting
    rain poltergeist salami
And a hundred tongues at once
Bumble Bee Heaven's my name
Cycling in graves
Little Joy Rider stuck her prehensile gibberish
Into the orbitic Tilt Mechanism freely bestowed by the papal party
That secretly seduced the swollen ash
From which six billion shadows stood up
Every dictator I've invented
And dried up the oceans

Drifting in my green dope cellar dream
Mother of black immaculates and sneezing scapulars
With the senatorial poets elect
With sting ray for breakfast
Juggling the clouds and weeping O the mystery of so many centuries

Art with its capitals
Imitating animal sounds
Went by
For this disquietudinous feather languishing infinity on a
    pedestal of shoes
All the images of Jesus were slapped together like Israel

And all was cool in the opium fields
Panama was stillborn from eagles of Hydra
There were so many birds bursting the hinges of Our Lady
She was hallucinated on the clever spot the Son chose
The Electric Decretal Caesar-christus

In and out of the valley of death
The valley of death
Little invisible bibles saying "How do you do, are the rare
    climates moldy today?"
Just then the surgeon general master initiate
Slunk from his vatlined shroud of history
Imhotep — Voltaire — his name —
Would you believe it?
I'm going to go to sleep

•

I shall say these things that curl beyond reach
A fatal balloon
Resolving riddles
It's pure abyss-crackling vortex

And silence opens her lips very much like arson

•

Tomb rise
And it sees a vision of beauteous sexual bags
And the caravan of flutes drops its melons over the sands I am not
Into the fog I am
The infinite I become
With mad hands scraping the jewel of my hideaway
To rise to the black pinnacle Roman empires of thought
Fly down fast and around Amitabha
A succession of literary images cabalas insecticides
Nail your heart here

Stone windows grate their teeth
And the processions are inside secret rooms
The death ravens chatter

I won't let the precision instruments bite me
I'm obsessed by death fantasies

There's this silken road
Down here I can invent the moth to kill memory
Flay it alive
With gasoline wings
There's another road out of these rooms
Into the streets of elegant gawkers
Cafés have electric chairs now
And this is no road to travel
And this is the road to oblivion happiness
Cutup on the unknown and another acre of poems

Musick?
Here come the flagons of Isidore Ducasse
The speed which is happening
                        And the grave compassion

            •

The riot was mainly in my mind
Soon I won't be here stretched out on pillows of imaginary iron
And the evil jinn leering into my dreams
I'm vanishing like vanishing letters
I can't bridge you reader you'll have to find yourself
Going on slow as the blood I see drop over us

           •

        Deflowering of technology
        Beauty the suicide
        Ice fevers
        Wrapped around your head
        Hers on fire

           •

Even if supersonic sounds feed me with ithyphallic diseases and
   the roars of Aboreas
Was plainchant less tedious?
Answer me

Don't just stand there like the Tetragrammaton
This is truth
I'm obsessed by death fantasies
Husks
And the *Night Thoughts* of Edward Young

Death is a pineapple in the cake of death
Which wing?
I deny death I don't know why
Ask the swans who are rocking me under the chair forest

The dragon I saw
Small as my Jupiter finger
Looking back with miniature flames
The whole middle ages
And vanish quickly
Beauteous apparition I was thinking of war A poem
Beauty must be reckoned with

The Romantic Movement

to Nancy

The boat tilts on your image on the waves between a fire of foam and the flower of moon rays, these the flags of your dreaming lips. I'm watching Venus on the ogred sky and a continent in cocoons.

Soon all the butterflies of desire shall manifest o prescience of life becoming poetic . . . and poetry the incense of the dream. A street and a forest interchange their clothing, *that* tree of telephones, *this* television of nuts and berries — the air edible music.

King Analogue
Queen Image
Prince Liberty . . .
. . . Garden of imperious images, life is a poem someday to be lived: the feast of our hearts on fire, the nerves supplying spice, blood coursing a glow of insects, our eyes the dahlias of torrential ignition.

The whisper of the inter-voice to wrap you in the mantle of marvelous power, with the secret protection of the forest that falls asleep in fire whose ores become transmined only for love — all your steps will lead to the inner sanctum none but you behold, your shadow putting on the body of metaphoric light.

The stone I have tossed into the air of chance shall come to you one great day and exfoliate the original scarab, the carbuncle of delights, the pomegranate inviolate, the sonorous handkerchief of the Comte de Saint-Germain, all the reinvented perfumes of ancient Egypt, the map of the earth in the Age of Libra when the air shall distribute our foods, the sempiternal spectrum of sundown at Segovia (the stork carrying the golden egg from the Templar's tower) Chief Seattle's lost medicine pouch, our simultaneous presence in all the capitals of Europe while traveling

Asia and listening to the million-throated choir of tropical birds, your lost candlewax empire, a madrone forest to live inside of, which we can wrap up in a set of "secret bags" and open on our wanderlust, the turbulent cry beneath the oceans, the extinct birdcalls in a magical vessel Christian Rosenkreuz dropped on his way out of Damcar, beads of coral dissolving the last motors, the redolent eyes of first-born seers, the key to the bank of sanity, the ship of honey at the height of storms through which we sail to new islands rising from the sunken continents and the bridge between sleep and waking we will traverse in constant possession of "the great secret" become transparent as a tear drop — *with no other work but the genius of present life.*

Bed of Sphinxes

A light opens as a street closes
against the bedrock of insistent glimmers
and your face talking to its cloud
Always the rinsings of milky flowers cry on the crest
where I'm a magnet gamboling with a drunken adept
There's a cloth of wine beneath us
the sugar of precipitous birds hands out rectangles of light
Racing out of town
the nerve-veined hair swallows the road

•

The verb cunningly made
traverses the shattered lamp
on the stockings' shimmering key
The plate over the doorway
swoons with miniature flames
impersonating what I'm handed out of shadows

The day heaving straw giants
if you can see them
expects me in a wet mirror
With the middling haste of quest
and further questions
rumbling at breakneck speed
the cortex of history looks through
the tubes of its material horizon

•

The hand and spoon
gather themselves into a turbulent cloudburst
before the latchkey from the advancing storm
takes leave of its gullies
with purple screams charging the table of water become
the ocean I hand you from an antelope beating
the stream of flies diagonal

to the fall of an empire and perpendicular
to the truss on fire with scimitars of breath

A war in the clothes closet is worth a panda on the moon
I am florescent
And you are a teardrop of infinite agate

Primavera

It is the oaken village that falls, splintered through a dust of visage where I gallop, no more flint than air, to think of cabalist hope: a universal alteration in the germination of planets.

But, the mystagogic chairs smashed in seed wars, I'm conceived again by the imponderables of total conjunction—even my shadow with another's that left its organs (sexploding suns) some distance from the translations of matter into an image.

This way the poem becomes an open sluice for darkness. Only the most obscure body is the brightest unity.

I catch hold of a train inside an iris.

Time at the window of maternal cosmetic, the high-heeled foot garlanded by a silken phallus spectates the forest where the uterine furnishings sink into drawers at bay from that twilight flashing in a mirror of dressing and undressing.

The preternatural identities beat the clouds from their barks, a child's chance look at the raging smolder of roses. Nearing sleep, this same wind rustles the void of blood-stained horses (my first cabals) whose galaxy dissolves *with a kiss* the victorious rescue of the palpable shadow streaming stars, her face: this bed, the undulant phantom: her hips.

We ride wooden horses
Always a desert marries the boiling water.

Becoming Visible

A whorl of happy eyes and devilish faces
struck out of antique sensuous paintings
twinkle from the knees and calves
moving slower than dream women

the hands are gesturing with violet blood
come from floating feathers
their sea anemone fingernails opening tropical fruits
(mango skins over snow)
and quickly rising to summer I meet you
walking in sateen boots over jewels of ice we spread for you

•

With the fox to see by
subterranean rivers advance
from under an asphalt sky
Auroras you exhale
the scorpion poem between our bellies
the mint's pebble trickles down the three-thousand-year-old flute
washed up on a lemon-leaf bed
the way your look born of mollusc tears
mirrors the fins of memory in a dolphin's eye

•

Ah that taste of liquid spoon
magnified from the forest's apple
and where your odors lie unfurling
comets' toes fire into orioles
(on their steps leave no traces)
twining my marrow's light
from your turning head of nervous lips
The stars dress up their furrows
whose divers sign you bathing
a torch of musk awakening my spark of fruit

In Yerba Buena

The brush is not the mortar

Red fog in the night

Across the valleys neon materializes
into shouts and descries the ogre in the manor house
(occulted though he is)
and the house in sweet flames
The flying parapet
has winced
three times the jolly crimes

Tomorrow
the black village will rise
with turrets of jimpson weed
engraved on a mockingbird's geometry

Beauty a great invisible
walks between luminous slabs
the better to blacken them
for the powers of the manticore
and the village which awaits him

It is the night and dawn of Robin Hood and Marian

The remains of sicilian flutes have docked
the archivists are pleased
Metallic brains alive!
lutes smashed on pavements of chicory
the climbing witnesses bang their heads
on far-flung empires of rain

Those natives called Ohlone
in the peculiar humors of the weather
and those who danced
to placate "The Great Invisible"
in the bay of Yerba Buena
    "dance on the brink of the world"

No reprieve for the ghost-catchers

Here the basaltic hieroglyphics of Sir Francis Drake
stream the lumens of California *"la maravillosa"*
Sequoia sempervirens
russet red
    vampire of wood
in you we have our being and move
who tolerate hardly a bird insect or other tree
but the woodpecker
    darting rattle of the air

Oraibi

What I mean when I say the key of the future is written now
    when it's seen
in the air of your great visage
an emblematic key
roaring
and with a wolf's expression
dashed on the ocean's knee

bear of lightning
in a black lanterned bay
smiling with the teeth of conch shells

What I'm saying when I tell you there's an orchard around my
    head
sprouting twenty-two engines of what will be
turning the blinding crystal
sight reading waves of fire
around the acentrical isle

What I'm doing now peering from invisible windows
and they also on fire
the wind masked as a moon
a hundred eighty letters volatilize into a forest of ocular organs

To read the green fire of lazy letters
truly of the metaphor's metaphor
the cabala rides through on a helmet
at the sight of the mountain
looking back at me
waving stones over a field of sleeping eyes

Oriabi: Literally "high rock," Hopi Indian village, Arizona, founded in the 12th century, the oldest continuously inhabited settlement in what is now the United States.

Obelisk at dawn
        obelisk at the crepuscular dawn
green corn makes a white butterfly
into an obelisk traveling at night
magnetic leaves of aurist fingers

What's written on the obelisk's petticoat
ventricles of wind hide
and reveal
        at the sovereignty of turquoise
intercepting great impossible cities
becoming visible
through the roads of the turquoise sun

Ultima Thule

The hoofs of sleep rattle from the blue whisper
of a crow plunged for sediment
gone beyond the frame whose disk flaunts the night's dawn

I fly into that marsh of brilliant gallop
the wheel within my hand
this glance of rain
sleep of sleep turning over stones the Lilliputians wake

Illusions of space vanish
where alone
          there are bodies only

Beyond This Trail of Crystal Rails

If I travel the leaves
planes of circling light cloy the branches
to skip by twigs and charge
like rhapsodes of pain
                  into sleep

gargantuan boulder harbinger
where the pen dips only brazen
and tails of solvent grace . . .
. . . The prismatic apple explodes
from this long-sought night
at the sight of you found on the limit
    of the returning forest
visibly crossing invisible dew

To Begin Then *Not Now*

The skylight drowns
as you walk into my voice
carrying a box of flames
entirely secretive
you tap open by the charmed hairpin
of the mysteries of sleep

Time Traveler's Potlatch

For Simon Rodia: The sudden appearance, at once, of a million Americans in Watts, in order to be in close proximity to his Towers.

For Charlie Parker: The materialization of his old green jacket re-forming the flag of the future republic of desire and dreams.

For Edgar Allan Poe: Upon awakening, an original copy of the *Manifeste du Surréalisme*.

For Charlie Chaplin: His wrench of *Modern Times* reconstituted as Merlin's magic wand.

For Bela Lugosi: A chance meeting with Morgan le Fay at the observation roof of the Empire State Building.

For William Collins: His "Ode to Fear" engraved in vanishing letters on the Scottish Highlands between the bleeding milk of night and the death wish of the coming day.

For Clément Magloire-Saint-Aude: The cinematic projection from a hummingbird's eye of Charlie Parker's spontaneous musical session at Bop City, San Francisco in 1954, fixed in an order of black, white and red crystallizations volatilizing the human brain on the brink of an evolutionary mutation through a circle of blazing rum.

Words I Dream

A gem with a head
a life on the brink
falling like a lute
through endless space
heart strings are felt
the wonderous look of invisible fish
drunk as sober is
the street a dream
no dreams in death
the outside inside
and the tediums of insufferable labor
Captain Stalin in Generalisimo Franco
believe me "the turn of things"
nightmare in a glass eye
smooth and simple as Milton's dictum
Sensuous spirit
the Babels of violence
I'll say it with sputniks and spuds of desire
on the loamy earth of the heart's desire
for the grandeurs of absolute equality
There's permission of persimmon
lore of my time

the gravitational pull of passionate wavelengths
a crack on the horizon
The fireworks of nostalgic festivals in Mexican villages
soothe the footsteps
up the city beneath the sea

There

on that chain of Ohlone mountains
shafts of light on a bobcat
through the thick madrones
first seen emblems that endure cupped my nine years
the great booming voice of nature
in the red bark's sloping labyrinth
who called my name
fetishes of pebbles and tabac in a redwood pouch
secret house of bark between the branches
these lights never die whose embers glow wilder
than wilderness at the beginning of words
to catch the ring of stars
                        at the still point
of infinite sur-rational flight
all was bathed in red
according to the perfection of temporal mirrors
elastic time in the gape of memory
visionary recitals in the exultant spring oblivious to the sea

Phi

"mystery of every day"
nothing has been written over nothing there's the title for the
    swan's game
there will be written never spoken in the horniest glade
forces are moving It was never done
There's the foam of its nothing that was never written heard in a
    gong without lips to speak it a horn it was peeking through X
the matter at hand
on the fire of the expanding cortex
there will be death there's no death in salt the lovers coalesce
never known how not to conceal
and yet light grows to a fifth seal
the rumpling waves of what is written
the pure blind beacons are the focus to the dream forest
to be read that has never been written

Isn't Poetry the Dream of Weapons?

The impossible is easy to reach
Who knows the way out of the labyrinth?
These are not rhetorical questions
the heart has its reasons though reasons not
                            Imaginary
the postmodern world has faded today
tomorrow, well shucks, it's here
a wedding calmly observed between heart and head
Relax the slow confusion flows until
the tooth of it
forgotten on a summer beach in Southern California
the way it's drawled to death in Southern California where death
    is cozy and Lemurian
Today I had my *tamasic* enlightenment the federation of anarchs
    was conspiratorially formed in Albania
the news came by indirect means the lines were jammed but I
    think I got it straight
here in the Far West you know how hard of hearing we are You've
    heard tell Ah'm sure
the clay hands looking a little moldy of Joaquin San Joaquin
the lazy simple status
nowhere to
and
always AND
Can this be the surprise statement
    Nuub
        nuub
            with high rhetoric back from bright death
what else to say of it?
No luck a metaphysical symbol
There's soaring even among the tortured minerals
These are the gilds of free verse
Doesn't the horror of writing Am I reading?
Better not to repeat you Sovereign Powers

the astral too plain at noon black with engines slipping again
five times
the secret hoarded afresh
Look at the basket now, my friend, *where* the fruits among the froth?
Between the ecstasy and the secret
I've touched bottom I want to be lost
the glow is bathing me in pain
the master would say, *souffrance*
Cosmic recurrence of the light of the old
its youth becoming
planting Dada on the trees
The within is without at once
no sooner dead than living
the unique perspective dangles the motion
it was called the boat of Ra
and the golden night hermetically sealed
        pure rollicking play
hands are glowing the last look back
lighted shadows like video
the words you see
pomegranate of idea
a pile of rust
Poetry knows in the unknowing
but *Kemi* is the moment to send up the aroma of dragons
beyond the limits salt of the sun
the deliberate anomaly willed by nexus
covers the filings I remember to forget dead to the sun
        Nescience
the sandpiper's ignition
Illuminate manuscripts explode through glass
your behemoth or mine
the salty bowels of Satan no less a shadow
the aquarian *pied-à-terre* this crocus of glittering mud island, the
   grebe's look, diving
transmutational obsidian
between Mount Konocti and Shasta
        across the boat of the sky people

But for love
there were new forms to birth
life was not
but for life only begun
among the various gleamings, light bearers, I met one and there
   are others at the heart of the mineral subject
It's the irrational factor
unraveling out of sight Joan Crawford at the heights the snarl of
   Dorian Gray *Comedia* of sleight of hand the velvet tissues
Watch the bean
               the Marvelous
in the wisp of wind rounding the corner at Carabeo where the
   magician had set up his rectangular table, hand and eye in the
   other
Today tropic birds in winter overhead as if I knew something
cubicles of wandering sound
wild parakeets to the lighthouse on the hill
This is the dream of the supernatural land
from rocking to it, what was once pain
is the bliss of it
The green demons with silvery genitalia rain down the flags of
   omnivorous pines
                      dilating light

Wilderness Sacred Wilderness

It's cozy to be a poet in a bed, on a copse, knoll, in a room
It's terrible to be a poet dragons around to bite off your wings
   and dream of the Standing One
as Nietzsche turns into Victor Emmanuel Re d'Italia
Helen Ennoia looks up into the eternal pools of the eyes of Simon
   Magus
and all the botched lies of mythic ties kick open the corpse a bag
   of museum dust
              manikin
in the manner of Simon Rodia, Buffalo Bill, like P.T. Barnum like
   Alka Seltzer
          goes against it
burnt pork eaters
El Dorado is the flashback to pancake mornings "home is where
   you hang yourself"
          signed Bill
The games of golf on the misogynist wastes
centuries multiply metaphysical field notes
There's the sleep of Ra in the West
a blurred photo of purple and lumens
on a windy hilltop in the manner of Man Ray
luminous sky my own poetry chimes at the horrid hour of hideous
   chimes
Poe's Appalachia in the far western sea where the forest saves us
   the forest hides us telepathines in a circle of friends
salacious hour of shadows regions of the undead
hangnails of the Gilak an infinite crystalline substance spun all the
   traditions
moored in nine powers the gurgling carburetors
the video cassettes the people are coming we're at
the communion on the mountaintop it's true but
the wheel turns the beaver chews the pole holding up the world

It's coming back home like a dream-memoir at the death of day in
 the poetical pastiche framing a mask of postcard view from the
 dawn of Ra
it's the moment of Maldoror
the collage objects of the end days conjunct the plutonic week a
 roadshow of nineteenth-century bison
as the Buffalo Bill Follies autodestruct by 1916

Native Medicine

Forty years ago I was born from a crumpled tower of immaculates
    that twist like the fleeting damaged bridge torrential rain on a
    road nearing Chehalis
                      love driving through her native land the
                      beauty
    of all I've received from her
the tears of an erotic Amonite sail Puget Sound to exalt the forest
    spirits we for whom all was Coyote made
the moments at Daladano our home in transfigured space
When I say love of the land I begin with native Amerindia:
Ohlones, Miwuk, Pomo, Ramaytush, Salinan
with the Washo peyotlists from the morning prayer in the bowl
    of dawn
none shall ever steal from me our sixty eyes to the smoke hole at
    the Tipi flue
embers of sacred earth — the myth has not lied —
a poor man like they — old in the vision of the floating tipi over
    the hideous towns below — once with the gods they say — but
    I'm no metaphysician, stop short at the crumble of dogmas —
the objects are prefigures of omniscient dew
the slash of cosmic jokery
corpses of the doomed sciences light the way against the rhetoric
    of anti-rhetoric and human misery true fault line of Birdy Dick
    "Old Grandmother"
I send up the song I could not sing this land my stony prayer
    people of human misery
Repetition shall not make it less than our hearts entwined
I am your mystery as you are there among the Pleiades
Ancient ones only you shall see us through
Serpent of suffering
they say there is nothing higher in the black grackle sounds at
    nightfall

Spumes

America in the Age of Gold

This one gives out he thinks poetry's at his beck and call
magic though proves it otherwise
even if adhered "spiritually"
soul whoppers gleam like solar rain
swift beaks of spring
golden automobiles in the muse's eye
the only darkness set in the distance
back to spectral Demo rotten mythologies stifle the air
thunders of the external world internalize
"and pay them no heed"
laying out the cards of triplicate dreams
always the future ruins of Coit Tower Manhattan African cities

From this north my head is full of you, Sur America
Sor Juana sailing the cloud her back to us from Mexico *real*
meeting John Donne in Arizona nearby the Penitentes are active
the massacres at Humboldt Bay later in the nineteenth century
recall now to memory
under the ruins of Brasilia
the red obsidian light of Church's *Cotapoxi*
siphon from the black marvelous swan in glass
the way trees revolve cosmic beauty
                Pine of diamond crest
                warblers of dew
Oak on the swollen breath at ocean
ancient wood my native land all this that vanishes

It's Blue Jay the doctor bird under cover of the silent machines
waits in the wind of Crow Raven Blackbird
ways the language leagues to bridge the polis
        sugar of the secessional forest city
the last utopia a mimesis like the tree monkey of Borneo
given to Mallard "the most beautiful of the Bird People"
for the Pomo there below Mount Konocti the home of Obsidian
  Man

to the whisper in the waterfall
There are many centers of mystic geography
but the great Black V of gold flashing in the meadow Bird
   unknown
opening the air like all the lore of the chants
        this may serve as shield
for the companions of the kestrel

At the green bowls green the revels of time
to step into orbs of the before time
wake up where the glyphs are lit within
with purest golden light
the Dawn-Bringer Meadowlark
the inner temple the forest temple
the American destiny line carries us to the Klamath meeting the
   ocean the river salmon spawn
Karuk of my dreams who dance the world renewal
the pentagonic flower of spring
legends of pine warblers
Junco of the most elegant suit
in a song of dynamic black and white
        alternate tones
harmonic wholes
      alcohols of
     the secondary powers

In the last wilderness of the mind
the chatter of world destruction below above the telepathic line
the minor key to the weather
the landscapes of Volney's ruins of empire
the expanding luminosity of Cole's Catskill paintings
I think of Cole at Burney Falls
Quidor at the Rogue River Rapids
the anonymous painter of *Meditation by the Sea* at Cape Arago on
   the secessionist coast
South channel to the riparian woods
all over Northern California still the end day imaginary land
lupines and poppies vegetable craters volcanic whispers

Wind ancient wind has hatched these Calafian landscapes
the sublime in the old sense
in the last days optic revolutions open the definitive end a forest
    to be
the irrational on a hindstone
Fata Morgana of the desolate strait
a hundred-mile wind and waves of violent ocean
There you drown send the death and with lumens belabor the
    straits surfaced to Shiva
She angelic tongue or not We're coming from the east to Celtic
    shores across the golden belt hanging the sights the flare of
    sand in the sea of dreams
wave of constant death the way red by chance comes forth
Antique language diagonal to intersections of time
south by northeast one with serpentine rock
warblers off nets the cliff-hanger's spell
birds so caped the skies in the time of the Karkins
to walk a living bridge of salmon
what was once joy with the supernatural beings
Gilak in the Pomo legend
That these spirits are here now with the clunk of material letters
the yellow-billed Magpie in the dry wind

Old nights of Bisbee the parades rolling back to Frisco
the Huachuca mountains inflected in a grossbeak
Copper blue rim of the rambling planet
across the *collini lombardini*
        1985 a number of antique
        printout somewhere primitive
        countryside of
        imaginary birds
The onrush of the western mythic image minute luminist
    transcription subverts the language the Canadian octophagic
    sails out of sight

The leader of a band of criminals
old Murrel It's good enough to skewer the waters
of the Natchez Trace There's sympathetic survival

early nineteenth-century outlaw of the wilderness
"Murrel's the finest"—"a wit of the wilds"—"a poet of predatory powers"

There's nary a Wilson but the warblers send cascades that wing the ears of Choctaws
Poetry magic love liberty
the unequivocally mediocre is an anti-meditation on bird houses
golden ringlets rare afternoons
the glade of theoric ornithic hermetica
a talon of deva dravidian bird
dæmon of legend
plucking the string
a diagonal of dew for the finches red-streaked
for the blush of the sun
the fifth note

Shasta

Against the current words came looking for me, the spark which evolves from *luz:* youth in the wind, tugboat in the bay, pollen lashes the gulfs of earthquake—laughing pilot, lingual lip sopping mineral waves—lost Aton hurtling forests down the atomic flue.

Steady the age, moon-signed zero minus zero year. Alexander Pope sabred the floxgloves. Whirlpool of Ys, the churning of divulgent scapes, everywhere the locus of dream. A jolly pencil in the void spins the tissue of stone. Graveyards of redwood root systems flavor salt systems going up river; the sparrows of summer launch pyres of rain.

Shasta great Shasta
Lemurian dream island, perhaps Atlantis, scallop on the sierra, Hopi sovereign of animate dream, oceanic claw: Alta California climbs into view.
Shasta great Shasta
geography in a mystic state later pruned by seers.

The return of the mad child molester, talking to him unravels the secrets of the Second World War. In the alchemical legends, there's a certain star seen at the completion of the Work, appears on the silver horizon through the trail in the grove. The languorous green dew strokes the burning red beam. The succulent pine resin writes kaleidoscopes between seasons.

The roads are closed by fire. The roads end, darken. Omens thicken, the psychic pain of being born. Only the blue vapor endures like sidereal weaving at the black seed, decay in the waters of the equestrian sea.

From the spiritualist masses of the nineteenth century, the flicker-feather collectors were defeated in rampant raids by inhuman hordes. Our ancestors born of the fruit fly are delusionary landscapes founded by autochthonal forces yet unknown. Wisps of *tankan* containing subatomic particles in the Azoth, the climbers mask the daemons where all was created . . . Transparent does lighten the prisms, ochres and green winds converge to interject the crossroads to the hooded figure . . . Apertures open to the Red Pepper Shaker . . . Silken inner tube — dream voice — is it you? Toxic filaments orison the radiant ebony idol.

Like a poet of the Phantom Empire, the roofer is tarring plutonian bones. By the melting computer stations, the power that was called up in the Fortean Society on Union Street drifts powders over the Lombard Steps. Hidden Marin to Mount Diablo in the east, first greetings from Blue Jay.

Rock power to the evanescent tabu-city sunlit on the leafy leather lizard of my hands — the madrone berry-lovers unfurl. Heat unravels the paradigm of a unique climatology of minds and few summer days auger the flame of Grip, a rider of rhododendrons to the north. I see chthonic man, and it's the wheel — the hated wheel — sending up a sliver of lucent dawn arched on a sunbeam serrating the vegetable stone: the light of her going by, a superior earth being, her clothes blued as a tissue of incandescent gold, something like an appearance of words — seen.

The fox spirits screech a pentacle for the fields drenched with flamboyant flagons, the baroque from all times, and flamenco barocco, as I leave you, Albion, gore of song: sempiternal dream curled in clouds of seashell, putrid cupids and the Black Fathers raping the wood nymphs of Nouvelle Bretagne.

The masked poets rise from the crumpled floor. The last aperture, reseen, glitters like a tortured cat. The flaming madrones are projecting the ballrooms of old Bisbee Arizona with Frisco *haut cuisine,* around the horns of unknown catastrophes for the Ohlones . . . The point is, the point is, the external Frisco scene is beginning to look like a 1928 *National Geographic* pinpointing Atlantic City, the European tourists wearing 1984

American-style, the marriage of Europe and North America, a locus of imminent sedition: Shasta from Suisun Bay north to the Rogue River; Frisco: diplomatic zone between IT and southern empires of regrettable memory

and LA-ba
    a special *là-bas* policy will prevail.

Poem for André Breton

When we met for the last time by chance, you were with Yves Tanguy whose blue eyes were the myth for all time, in the autumn of 1944
Daylight tubes stretched to masonry on Fifth and Fifty-Seventh in the logos of onomatopoeic languages of autochthonic peoples
Never have I beheld the Everglades less dimly than today dreaming the Ode to André Breton, you who surpassed all in the tasty knowables of Charles Fourier
Only the great calumet pipe for both of you We are hidden by stars and tars of this time
No one had glimpsed you great poet of my time But the look of your eyes in the horizon of northern fires turning verbal at Strawberry California
the Sierra Nevada seen from Mount Diablo on the rare clear day is enough of a gift to hold up over the rivers of noise
Metallic salt flies free
that "the state of grace" is never fallen
that the psychonic entities are oak leaves burnished with mysteries of marvelous love whose powers wake you with the glyph of geometric odors flaring in the siroccos about to return to Africa
Mousterian flint stones caress the airs of Timbuctu as I turn a corner of volcanic sunsets from the latest eruption of Mount Saint Helens

Ex Cathedra

To weave garter belts with chaos and snakes, the nun's toenail
 of crimson phallus, her breast of alligator, her tail, crow's
 buttocks. Steel pricks of the ciborium dovetail her white
 pantaloons — snake oil on a eucharistic tongue.

In crystal movies: an owl's path beneath slumbers of the woods
 that died to bolster the miserable stations of the cross, instead
 of Bugs Bunny laminating the hedgerows through the pews,
 stench gathers power in censers of the debasing perfumes.

Time of frostbites laid over crumbs of bile-soaked christies,
 famines roasted with divinity, allah jacks up his "prisons within
 prisons," the flayed kaaba-stone pitched to the solar gobbling
 machine.

After the Great Dusting, this Pope exhibits his toes in carnivals
 sure to spring up in sideshows of enigma, hot flints of the
 anti-christ, my brother, in lesions of the darkening space,
 Revolution the Star in the West springs the play of foam
 on the rocks below. . . .

Field mice from the mouths of "the hell sermon," I lop off the
 head of the oldest nun with a fragment of the reforgeable
 brassy metallic cross; this priest whipping Sister Matilda with
 guts spilled from the monstrance his tongue laps up at her feet.
 Oh, junkyards of eternity fester in leads of clock time, but
 Humankind invents the bomb I hurl to *The Box of Infanticides,*
 Black-hearted children flee gehenna, pissing through mountains
 of priestly corpses, those burnt hams in the tree of winds.

Schools of fish move in the night, plagues of scripture blown to
 smithereens.
Secret rooms fly open absolutely by stealth.
The star card bestows the charm of new rivers, this word
 tomorrow, Andromeda, and with you, Amor.

With the skull splendors of the imperium romanum, the alchemical
 pope skewers a host of puffers on the backsides of saints.
Cardinals butcher in the market day for clerics.
Inside the chalice of battered gums, the vengeance of witches,
 salmons to spawn the invisible eruption in the Street of the
 Five Rats.
Talismanic, the marigold's not a wing-feather less!

From the stone bubbles of Mother Angelica a herd of corpses
 rides to the spider compass of my bones: the blood of swans
 lace my handcuffs floating the altars, the inebriate sickle quick
 to slice those melting emeralds inlaid with scripted shit the
 great unknown rages to fruition on the flanks of Carthago.

The absolute pulverization of all the churches will be the grace of
 love's freedom!
On that day black holes of thought radiate the wind's lost word,
 this death that is not death: that day is magic is love.

Unachieved

Compared to the transcendental realm, the world under the
   roofed-in-cave is somber
but the colors, signatures
five senses and the sixth, their purifier
               touch by imagination's feather
       sight & sound of liquid flight from those waters the spirit
scrys

Beauty comes to it at the heart's desire
to transmute out of pleasure's pleasure a distillation of birds into
   visionary symbols
the processional of variable coloration of finches, choral lights,
that and the shadow we brood

I, in the wild state, inner feelings soar
Transcendence the mental dance imagines, but for an instant, as
   the poet Bryant returning to stone
                       The starry sky, Pluto's mirror
the way you could talk about your life, splinters off a
   carpenter's floor under a microscope, those perfect symmetries
   or better, visible shavings, but never the tool
Invisible something may strike through the black room of higher
   perfection
self-torture in the humanisphere a sure thing before a whole forest
   revolves to sign a bioregional imperative
consensus of the Hopi Way Separatist communes of no more than
   three thousand souls
                Dianas out of Gaea's caves
this window does not fade from view in the coming pre-industrial
   age
retrieved in a narrow shoal where a Gull Feather given in bliss
   turns the deranged corpse in ritual passes
healing prayers legitimize to exorcize the sick stain of being that
   death, die, at sight of the Androgynous Republic

Drums of magic, *salve,*
                      caught here
to return to the caesura, the interrupted fault line Frisco day
   which tunnels thought
Every time I think I'll turn off the main vein, quotidian concerns
   take over initiating script where you cut it, different than
   esoteric cant
but lingually deeper into it, like "cut it" in sacred science

. . . this flow of thought is different for the surrealist than for the
   rationalist diehard
Emotion signs this pain you're at the terminal syndrome Fabulous
   tunnels turn inner to bring up The Transcendent World Anew
   (it's never what you thought it was)
What I'm getting at is, why don't you examine with great care
   your entire body of death?
                      and
reorient the auditor to a gnosis so mystical the tree bark from
   which it claws refuses to inscribe whiteness
One with the supreme ego
                      nothing more elegant on the avian
   plane
flicker mandibles arrange the dwelling
and from all the gifts of Gaea, head for their origin:

> In my dream, the Goddess in her heavenly palace on the
>   earth
> a kind of Marienbad in lunar light
> She in her silver gown slightly décolleté
> has me watch the Stellar Mirror
> while stars of the Pleiades run in a rhythm of Eight
> and do an astral dance, *tout court*

Thus begins it, Love, she and the avatar in the Bo-Tree Garden
and consider from where I'm situated here in the Far West

               green lightning at Thunder's coast
looking east to Pharaonic Egypt where the West began

                bonsai trees among the pines
a swan's luminous power in air of mist

              haunted redwood shadows
world immortal because AMOR wove a tissue clear to specular sight
Wings of this city
                an otherwise haunted hillscape
                    ultimate Ys
Frisco once also covered with ancient waves
a kind of lost Atlantis several kalpas ago
its seven hills imagine old traditions of jazz

                Harmony is that secret
between the machines coming through Death is that machine
the wild wee drop
                    snow to the solar radiant a fumbled perfected
   Rebus of mental luminoids
                      music married to meaning when
   the orange
almost red-streaked crest
magnifies millet
                to mark off the duration:
Ornithos
        gold
        a parabola
                The treasure perch is you and me, love
a tiny winged fiery tongue through the green window
                            Forms are
   weddings
that spring trays of meaning between chirps
flutes garner ellipses of word
fork between eclipses of comet lore across lagoons

                salt
from the Mediterranean Sea fixed here at Nova Albion
A boy painting earth colors above the valley town
my first poetry atop San Bruno Mountain was all power ekstasis
as if all tracks had left the last railway station

the sensation of sudden union with another attraction
to decipher no matter what suffering there's no pain at the taste that tells an epic begins
brown & red over the mental rainbow
not to close this grandeur beyond words?
War mental war and no other These the weapons on the highest nest Golden V sang to Violent Ocean
It was forbidden to know what the melting glyphs said over the horizon
the ways down in the valley flowed away like darkness painting poetry to light
At this stage of the great game you can assassinate all the stand-ins with cosmic disdain *El Poder del Niño Jesus*
In the dreams of the Philippine "master" late of Frisco gone to Alaska
"Joke's on you" The Plague reminds The Fluke
Grey cant explosions through cells
prisons rent to specular essence
where it counts . . . is it laughter?
The old necromancer calls 'em up every day faster than thought Ibis eye of the Sacred Geomant
Gaea doing this dance down on the plain
coming of the inland sea where once there was none
I begin to steal Gaea
but Gaea is another circle of the rose Pantheism of the moment where all rivers meet from the mountaintop

Thunder for Gaea who's more than thunder
mysterious as in the beginning
Gaea the more I say you the seldom I leap through you
to my own ego
              upon the bread your birds beak

Diana Green

Of that spider weaving reality I can't speak
to pink it up under paper
riding away on invisible webs stopped by specular turns
These tiny living things happen to the King in his Bath
digression to a strange unhealthy place the first seen Great-tailed
    Grackle signifies mandibles true north

        "Could he be serious about all those esoteric ideas?"
that resolve everything into dust whose remains are alkaline salt
Go read it with supernatural teeth muttering a winged language
What if it were the moment before the perfect whole?

Watching months of decadence go by
Pluto retrograde five degrees into Scorpio "It's nothing, just an
    appearance"
        Several hundred million humans
billions of birds
would have fried if a second space shuttle had been launched after
    the first auto-destructed
What is shows up   galloping the inner image   the finest
    mirror to the absolute clock across a sunlit room buttercup
    wild thistles reeds and fruity trees where once there was only
    Crissy Field
        From the femur bones of language there'll be
    nineteen varieties
of Oak to meet you any day of the week "The skeleton of solitude"
    once writ is writ again
and the temple of Luxor goes over it in a transparency to catch it
    before it goes A Vision of Synarchic Bioregions over Northern
    California's haunted scapes
        Redwood powers in those fires across the Bay
up river to Mount Shasta
        and below the Oregon Caves
I've become this sublimating hand attuned to a darkness of

    sudden light on simulacra: the Great Green Faery Head thrust
    from redwood roots in the Humboldt Woods
                              luminist sheen

with the wrap of words penetrating wood
I like the old legend: this paper writes me working from
   predetermined
      feathers
         a mancy of chance
               delivered by Necessity
                      from the Mistress of the Birds
When we knew her under giant ferns Madumba's world from an
   ocean of her crystal palace
This calls for an Ode a Dawn Feast
Red-faced Cormorant will be there Magnificent Frigate Bird and
   the Red-Crowned of all species This imaginary avifauna
     suggests more terror before ritual indents a world indeed
meditated from a bow string
to speak a visible language
when you began   where you'll end   to begin again   Preserving
   fire
What moves the aging man closing a car door going slowly up to
   a metal gate
     The alchemic lesson after seeing what "Steal fire" means
                   Geometry is that key
         older than Paleolithic
         Attar's birds to the sun
I lean to that philosophic fire in caves   seashells   in the slow
   stalagmatic of geologic light
              Surface only is ours to see below Reason
                             reflect the Black Sun

             Every autumn Nature has a way of showing that
   dragon-knot of iridescent rot
Any forest sends up a message
             clear   non-occulted   lux of darkness
                green ogre of putrefactional life Poets are
                speleologists at best

        to see on rocks off shore The Language of the Birds

     The clear-obscure of symbolical tropes
        zings cosmic pleasures of laryngeal thought

Become my own cave? No easy matter   There's a reversal of
   those actions which may turn into gestures "These things I'm
   talkin' about"
Why not dare the despised? No sooner done than asked

Precious stones dance in a ring to distinguish a redpoll's song
   from the local finches
       (see to it, mercurial eminence, resolve it by contraries)
Fierce wild beings presage our transformation into salt — the
   whole past burnt into a phoenix nest — and leave a way open
   even if the smallest   whatever great took off long ago

      The horizon's turned over to read the *medu-Neter*
      The great crystal pool Starry Night breaks into caves
      There's such a sky   instant colorations   green to
                              magenta
     harmonic doubles of ascending letters
        dropped with leaf life
to the fogs of midsummer Doors expressionists slam An attempt
   to photoreal insomnia
There's no closure, sweetbrier Heightened teeth   for the vowel's
   intent from whence it situates
transmutable power

     a hand too languorous for drawing

this palm of oneiromancy can be read for thought, *if thought,* is
   diamond dust
"In harmless radioactive fallout"
on the way to the Rainbow Café
between the harmony of Clashing Rocks
there's a marsh and a meadow to call back the beasts
     "Your love affair with the birds"

Again the quintessential multicolored wild finches chirp 'round a
    tunnel an aerial way through the great game
Talking about divine emptiness (idiot-maniacal) I'm interlocking
    chips from memory's arcane shift to it
        Mirror specks devolve
to the Labyrinth Sacrifice seems sempiternal There's something
    about the ecstatic virgins of sacrifice that ties into our Subject
    when finches land swiftly
to fold out synesthetical displays at the brink of the world That
    tribelet's misnomer, "Ohlone"
        mystery of holding a banner a stream of that next
    corner around a trail into redwood bark to imagine
bubbling beer of manzanita berries when Coyote made love to
    thousands of Dianas

Proportional to the salt of the myth
Orpheus has the ticket from Daladano to the unique Fern Forest
    fronting Violent Ocean

        Spirit of transfigured space
        perfect equipoise
from having traveled to find and to have found it Poor Medium
There's hard-headed search for it among pebbles
radishes of crooked streets
marbles with knickers a naturalist in English woods of the 1920s
        between vectors but dreaming
and isn't it with daydreams that poetry begins to dance?

        Over Land's End touch Terra with your toes

        Someday to hear poetry from a cave
as the poetry of caves ignites all centers of Gaea's embers of new
    light
Given that flutter of sparrow wings to the tree
        Isis
        Diana
other nameless names
crossing over dimly with portmanteau Down channel

the way so fogged meeting all that which opposes itself *Coagula* at Crystal Lake rock castles of green shadows and the flaming dragon completes a torment *That was you, ISIS*

in Diana's glass   the birds

Egypt

In honor of R. A. Schwaller de Lubicz

Water   lustre of fire   this Hapy, this Nile
cobra skin dangles
from a crevice of a wall in the Apet Temple
stillness   soft sand   rustling breeze
Reading images around papyrus-fluted colonnades
— these moments wonder the world —
the hermetic secret   Plato   Pythagoras   Moses
finally, the Companions of Horus
come into view as the Resurrection Band
Music! perfumes! magic!

Risen, diagonally, from sun-bent water
to a green snake of trees, the Hoopoe bird
inflames gold-tinted air over the Nile
Each plumed locket on its redolent necklace
calls up spirits of the Libyan desert
I lay this baggage   to unravel   as this bird
          that confounds us   You're the vowel "O"
of the higher *ka* looking to the flowers in Amenti
Kingfishers dive from the people's ferry boat

Over there, the green western bank of the Hapy,
wandering egrets scan the object
of Nut's function to carry us through the netherworld
Fire preserves its season
to become a green flame of the living face of Egypt,
sequence of a visioned recital memory's
framed revelation musics to sight
Seeds in water open the book of black silt
Hoopoe with bands of Geb's brown tones
black as Kemi is to those indwelled by light

Predawn, the fellaheen saunter to their gardens
from non-electric   amber-lit   red brick houses

so silent, slow, lifting wooden hoes over rustic *gallabeyas*
    it could be the Eighteenth Pharaonic Dynasty
Gemmed, caught up in the old ways, silver flesh
gleams between mandibles of the African Kingfisher
These moving realities appear on the Nile
as if a postcard view of it held up a hieratic bird
       silent tonalities   a secret passage   the beginning of language
crowns   caps   flight of Wagtails   Hoopoes
              and the unknown at Karnak

Into the Dwat   gone into the Dwat
supernatural beings somewhere become vanished Horian light
       It's said   the Port
       driest of earth sand
       between powders of the Two Places
       as we come to them from a difficult crossing
       on to a way of practical harmony with the breath of virtual
       plants

Another day to write you out,
the second time round, forms pronounce
and gambol over to become phonic discretions
In the sepulchre of a sempiternal King
sometime between the Seventh and Eighth Hours
we view the circular intervals
double twelve on the stone ceiling
There was light at the end of the narrow passageway
to the Covered inner chambers of the Temple
At the invisible door of gold, Earth's lover
by a mirror seen   Better to go to the Dwat conscious
following dawn to dusk   joy   wind   and the branches thereof
Be calmed from the western horizon at Waset
The proof's in being there
Fourfold curtains drift dry to indigo
      nine blue herons on the horizon read from right to left
scent dimly recalls an unction savored in the Twenty-fifth Dynasty
      Interruptions will be solutions
      forfeiting the so-called fourth dimension

and if this evil goes into particles:
return to the supine in serpentine form

There's an inhalation of dawn's dew
a boat furled to the Red Sun opening and closing
those horizons that are Egypt

It's easy to hallucinate Edgar Allan Poe
sipping Turkish coffee, *mazbout,* at Groppi's on the Talat Harb
Nineteenth-century Italianate masonry curling a corner
of endless newspapers of the world
The Oudj Eye multiplies invisibly
Horus visibly wears a Falcon's Head
become visible within crepuscular shadows at the nightfall of the
    world
whose matrix is Cairo

Reminiscing Heliopolis, ancient On of the North,
the winged shadow of the Sphinx
and all shadows between lit-up visuals
through the dream-veined streets
frame the great signature
that is eternal Egypt
            KMT Kemi the Black

from which this and the Mirror ☥ hath come . . .

From a sojourn on the Nile (Hapy), Autumn, 1989

*Passionate Ornithology Is
Another Kind of Yoga*

       Thirty feisty finches at the window   FINCHDOM
Four or five double-tufted crowns
Midsummer   Spring-born
most daring of the lot   clumsy but quick
at our plastic feeder tray
Beata framed nude at a door
points her Jupiter finger: Rarely seen
a White-crowned sparrow gets blown away
by these non-Kropotkin red   yellow
silver   orange birds
                They're mean
never give any sparrow (though higher
on the taxonomic tree) even a mite's chance
to beak powder flecks finches drop
while scarfing up their hulled sunflower seeds

                •

Glass shadows a suprasensual object
become a secret shuttle
down an escalator going simultaneously up
"the one and only god" found
from that dawn and night on the Nile
           space
where all ends in a beginning
           Amenti
mutating roseate to indigo tint
behind the darkening horizon
Over to the River's other side
my hidden eye of Horus sights
one old jazz record repeated
myriad nights & days
on a plane gathering Bird and Mozart
distant Vivaldi, wild music of
contrasting flowers whose tones

interject this Ohlonian Spring of
superfinches I love more than to become a star
Ah   visible angels of superior affectivity
with the most perfect language of sight
The chosen Red-plumed seeder
ritually feeding the Silver-lined
and a chorus of them form
an unpremeditated pentacle of erotic song

•

So few of us
if the seed be
become scythe, its own end
as wheaten being
germinates a songbird's form
We, too, were once avian
bridge — window — to another life
So they do know us
though now in terror
A few listen with attention —
instant Ornithos, rare
flashing cordial of communicating grace —
who see what I imagine they become
Their gestures speak with deep silence,
flying hearts, before they take off
and primordial gnosis takes flight
to carry seeded mandibles on the wind
who are clothed in primary colors
range, breadth and tones of what
red streamed from
Then, branching leaves envelope
perching forms beneath
a swathe of indigo

Index of Titles, First Lines
Titles appear in italics

Ambivalent miles, sorceries played, 31
A Civil World, 11
A gem with a head, 109
A light opens as a street closes, 97
A soul drenched in the milk of marble, 3
A whorl of happy eyes and devilish faces, 100
A window that never ends, 21
A Winter Day, 9
Against the current words came looking for me, 122
America in the Age of Gold, 118
Ancients Have Returned Among Us, 70
And the sea moved over the terrace, 87
Animal Snared in His Revery, 26
[As some light fell], 38
As the women who live within each other's bodies, 19
Astro-Mancy, 77
At halls of Oedipus blind, 53
Automatic World, 7
Awakened From Sleep, 15
Ball, 41
Becoming Visible, 100
Bed of Sphinxes, 98
Beyond This Trail of Crystal Rails, 106
Blue Grace, 68
Blue Locus, 81
By the window cut in half Jeanlu, 63
Coat of Arms, 79
Compared to the transcendental realm, 128
Dead Smoke, 31
Deamin, 54
Diana Green, 132
Egypt, 137
Ephemeris, 85
Ex Cathedra, 126
Fantast, 88
Fin del Mundo, 51

Flaming Teeth, 90
For Simon Rodia: The sudden appearance at once, 108
Forty years ago I was born from a crumpled tower of immaculates, 117
From a jet plane window I landed into an 18th-century drawing room, 88
From the Front, 56
Go! my calf-headed drone! 64
He breathes through his wounds, 26
Hermetic Bird, 5
High, 62
Horse Angel, 89
How depressing here I am after my nerves tonged hell!, 65
Hypodermic Light, 46
I Am Coming, 22
I am following her to the wavering moon, 22
I have given fair warning, 60
I hear him, see him—interpenetrate, 27
I touch you with my eyes, 83
I walked you sank you in black glass, 39
If I travel the leaves, 106
If you are bound for the sun's empty plum, 23
[Iguana, Iguana], 35
[In a grove], 42
In a moment their faces will be visible, 11
In the rose creeping into the tower of exiles, 9
In Yerba Buena, 101
Infernal Landscape, 21
Infernal Muses, 64
Inside the Journey, 24
Interior Suck of the Night, 34
Isn't Poetry the Dream of Weapons, 112
It is I who create the world and put it to rest, 43

It is the oaken village that falls, 99
It's absurd I can't bring my soul to the eye of odoriferous fire, 46
It's cozy to be a poet in a bed, on a copse, knoll, in a room, 115
It's here the glove attacks the hand, 81
[It's summer's moment in autumn's hour], 40
Jeanlu, 63
Luminous, 83
Mirror and Heart, 118
[Man is in pain], 28
Morning Light Song, 61
Mystery of every day, 111
Narcotic air simple as a cone, 34
Native Medicine, 117
O beato solitudo! where have I flown to?, 62
Observatory, 36
Of that spider weaving reality I can't speak, 132
On that chain of Ohlone mountains, 110
Only for those who love is dawn visible throughout the day, 82
Oraibi, 103
Out of My Hat of Shoals, 86
Passionate Ornithology Is Another Kind of Yoga, 140
Phi, 111
Plumage of Recognition, 3
Poem for André Breton, 125
Primavera, 99
Pure as gale and mist washing my skull, 79
Quickly, I rocked between waves, 24
Red Dawn clouds coming up!, 61
Resurrections, 42
Rompi, 67
Sea towers of Sicily, 75
Shasta, 122
She Speaks the Morning's Filigree, 72
Sheri, 39
Smoke tilts in space, 36
Still Poems, 58
Subconscious Mexico City New York, 65
Swept from the clouds, 15

Talisman, The, 82
Tenochtitlan!, 56
Terror Conduction, 29
The Analog, 87
The boat tilts on your image, 95
The brush is not the mortar, 101
The Diabolic Condition, 19
The earthquake slivers, 90
The Enormous Window, 13
The hoofs of sleep rattle from the blue whisper, 105
The impossible is easy to reach, 112
The menacing machine turns on and off, 29
The mermaids have come to the desert, 1
The night is a space of white marble, 59
The Owl, 27
The poem says the bombs of America went off, 51
The Romantic Movement, 95
The room has lips to speak antediluvian wishes, 85
The skylight drowns, 107
The stars have gone crazy, 77
The sun has drowned, 7
The teacups shattered upon the legs of ancient lovers, 17
The Wheel, 53
There, 110
There Are Many Pathways to the Garden, 23
There is this distance between me and what I see, 60
Thirty feisty finches at the window, 140
This is the grey limit, 58
This one gives out he thinks poetry's at his beck and call, 118
This silence doors shut against animals, spirits, 58
This sky is to be opened, 5
This word or this image, 89
Through the Night on Fire with My Blood, 72
Time Traveler's Potlatch, 108
To Begin Then Not Now, 107

This silence doors shut against animals, spirits, 58
This sky is to be opened, 5
This word or this image, 89
Through the Night on Fire with My Blood, 72
Time Traveler's Potlatch, 108
To Begin Then Not Now, 107
To weave garter belts with chaos and snakes, 126
Touch of the Marvelous, 1
Ultima Thule, 105
Unachieved, 128
U.S.S. San Francisco, 48
Vacuous suburbs, 58
Voice of Earth Mediums, 74
Water   lustre of fire   this Hapy, this Nile, 137
We are truly fed up, 74
What are you watching I am watching, 54
What I mean when I say the key of the future is written now, 103
What Is Not Strange?, 75
[What made tarot cards and fleurs-de-lis], 32
When we met for the last time by chance, 125
Where earth dropped into sun, 41
Wilderness Sacred Wilderness, 115
Within closets filled with nebulae, 13
Words I Dream, 109

CITY LIGHTS PUBLICATIONS

Acosta, Juvenal, ed. LIGHT FROM A NEARBY WINDOW: Contemporary Mexican Poetry
Alberti, Rafael. CONCERNING THE ANGELS
Alcalay, Ammiel, ed. KEYS TO THE GARDEN: New Israeli Writing
Allen, Roberta. AMAZON DREAM
Angulo de, G. & J. JAIME IN TAOS
Angulo, Jaime de. INDIANS IN OVERALLS
Artaud, Antonin. ARTAUD ANTHOLOGY
Bataille, Georges. EROTISM: Death and Sensuality
Bataille, Georges. THE IMPOSSIBLE
Bataille, Georges. STORY OF THE EYE
Bataille, Georges. THE TEARS OF EROS
Baudelaire, Charles. TWENTY PROSE POEMS
Blake, N., Rinder, L., & A. Scholder, eds. IN A DIFFERENT LIGHT: Visual Culture, Sexual Culture, Queer Practice
Blanco, Alberto. DAWN OF THE SENSES: Selected Poems
Bowles, Paul. A HUNDRED CAMELS IN THE COURTYARD
Breton, André. ANTHOLOGY OF BLACK HUMOR
Bramly, Serge. MACUMBA: The Teachings of Maria-José, Mother of the Gods
Brook, James & Iain A. Boal. RESISTING THE VIRTUAL LIFE: Culture and Politics of Information
Broughton, James. COMING UNBUTTONED
Broughton, James. MAKING LIGHT OF IT
Brown, Rebecca. ANNIE OAKLEY'S GIRL
Brown, Rebecca. THE TERRIBLE GIRLS
Bukowski, Charles. THE MOST BEAUTIFUL WOMAN IN TOWN
Bukowski, Charles. NOTES OF A DIRTY OLD MAN
Bukowski, Charles. TALES OF ORDINARY MADNESS
Burroughs, William S. THE BURROUGHS FILE
Burroughs, William S. THE YAGE LETTERS
Cassady, Neal. THE FIRST THIRD
Churchill, Ward. A LITTLE MATTER OF GENOCIDE
CITY LIGHTS REVIEW #2: AIDS & the Arts
CITY LIGHTS REVIEW #3: Media and Propaganda
CITY LIGHTS REVIEW #4: Literature / Politics / Ecology
Cocteau, Jean. THE WHITE BOOK (LE LIVRE BLANC)
Cornford, Adam. ANIMATIONS
Corso, Gregory. GASOLINE
Cuadros, Gil. CITY OF GOD
Daumal, René. THE POWERS OF THE WORD
David-Neel, Alexandra. SECRET ORAL TEACHINGS IN TIBETAN BUDDHIST SECTS
Deleuze, Gilles. SPINOZA: Practical Philosophy
Dick, Leslie. KICKING
Dick, Leslie. WITHOUT FALLING
di Prima, Diane. PIECES OF A SONG: Selected Poems
Doolittle, Hilda (H.D.). NOTES ON THOUGHT & VISION
Ducornet, Rikki. ENTERING FIRE
Eberhardt, Isabelle. DEPARTURES: Selected Writings
Eberhardt, Isabelle. THE OBLIVION SEEKERS

Eidus, Janice. VITO LOVES GERALDINE
Fenollosa, Ernest. CHINESE WRITTEN CHARACTER AS A
   MEDIUM FOR POETRY
Ferlinghetti, L. ed. CITY LIGHTS POCKET POETS ANTHOLOGY
Ferlinghetti, L., ed. ENDS & BEGINNINGS (City Lights Review #6)
Ferlinghetti, L. PICTURES OF THE GONE WORLD
Finley, Karen. SHOCK TREATMENT
Ford, Charles Henri. OUT OF THE LABYRINTH: Selected Poems
Franzen, Cola, transl. POEMS OF ARAB ANDALUSIA
García Lorca, Federico. BARBAROUS NIGHTS: Legends & Plays
García Lorca, Federico. ODE TO WALT WHITMAN & OTHER
   POEMS
García Lorca, Federico. POEM OF THE DEEP SONG
Garon, Paul. BLUES & THE POETIC SPIRIT
Gil de Biedma, Jaime. LONGING: SELECTED POEMS
Ginsberg, Allen. THE FALL OF AMERICA
Ginsberg, Allen. HOWL & OTHER POEMS
Ginsberg, Allen. KADDISH & OTHER POEMS
Ginsberg, Allen. MIND BREATHS
Ginsberg, Allen. PLANET NEWS
Ginsberg, Allen. PLUTONIAN ODE
Ginsberg, Allen. REALITY SANDWICHES
Goethe, J. W. von. TALES FOR TRANSFORMATION
Gómez-Peña, Guillermo. THE NEW WORLD BORDER
Harryman, Carla. THERE NEVER WAS A ROSE WITHOUT
   A THORN
Heider, Ulrike. ANARCHISM: Left Right & Green
Herron, Don. THE DASHIELL HAMMETT TOUR: A Guidebook
Herron, Don. THE LITERARY WORLD OF SAN FRANCISCO
Higman, Perry, tr. LOVE POEMS FROM SPAIN AND SPANISH
   AMERICA
Jaffe, Harold. EROS: ANTI-EROS
Jenkins, Edith. AGAINST A FIELD SINISTER
Katzenberger, Elaine, ed. FIRST WORLD, HA HA HA!: The Zapatista
   Challenge
Kerouac, Jack. BOOK OF DREAMS
Kerouac, Jack. POMES ALL SIZES
Kerouac, Jack. SCATTERED POEMS
Kerouac, Jack. SCRIPTURE OF THE GOLDEN ETERNITY
Lacarrière, Jacques. THE GNOSTICS
La Duke, Betty. COMPAÑERAS
La Loca. ADVENTURES ON THE ISLE OF ADOLESCENCE
Lamantia, Philip. BED OF SPHINXES: SELECTED POEMS
Lamantia, Philip. MEADOWLARK WEST
Laughlin, James. SELECTED POEMS: 1935–1985
Laure. THE COLLECTED WRITINGS
Le Brun, Annie. SADE: On the Brink of the Abyss
Mackey, Nathaniel. SCHOOL OF UDHRA
Masereel, Frans. PASSIONATE JOURNEY
Mayakovsky, Vladimir. LISTEN! EARLY POEMS
Mrabet, Mohammed. THE BOY WHO SET THE FIRE
Mrabet, Mohammed. THE LEMON
Mrabet, Mohammed. LOVE WITH A FEW HAIRS

Mrabet, Mohammed. M'HASHISH
Murguía, A. & B. Paschke, eds. VOLCAN: Poems from Central America
Murillo, Rosario. ANGEL IN THE DELUGE
Nadir, Shams. THE ASTROLABE OF THE SEA
Parenti, Michael. AGAINST EMPIRE
Parenti, Michael. DIRTY TRUTHS
Pasolini, Pier Paolo. ROMAN POEMS
Pessoa, Fernando. ALWAYS ASTONISHED
Peters, Nancy J., ed. WAR AFTER WAR (City Lights Review #5)
Poe, Edgar Allan. THE UNKNOWN POE
Porta, Antonio. KISSES FROM ANOTHER DREAM
Prévert, Jacques. PAROLES
Purdy, James. THE CANDLES OF YOUR EYES
Purdy, James. GARMENTS THE LIVING WEAR
Purdy, James. IN A SHALLOW GRAVE
Purdy, James. OUT WITH THE STARS
Rachlin, Nahid. THE HEART'S DESIRE
Rachlin, Nahid. MARRIED TO A STRANGER
Rachlin, Nahid. VEILS: SHORT STORIES
Reed, Jeremy. DELIRIUM: An Interpretation of Arthur Rimbaud
Reed, Jeremy. RED-HAIRED ANDROID
Rey Rosa, Rodrigo. THE BEGGAR'S KNIFE
Rey Rosa, Rodrigo. DUST ON HER TONGUE
Rigaud, Milo. SECRETS OF VOODOO
Ross, Dorien. RETURNING TO A
Ruy Sánchez, Alberto. MOGADOR
Saadawi, Nawal El. MEMOIRS OF A WOMAN DOCTOR
Sawyer-Lauçanno, Christopher, transl. THE DESTRUCTION OF
    THE JAGUAR
Scholder, Amy, ed. CRITICAL CONDITION: Women on the Edge
    of Violence
Sclauzero, Mariarosa. MARLENE
Serge, Victor. RESISTANCE
Shepard, Sam. MOTEL CHRONICLES
Shepard, Sam. FOOL FOR LOVE & THE SAD LAMENT OF
    PECOS BILL
Smith, Michael. IT A COME
Snyder, Gary. THE OLD WAYS
Solnit, Rebecca. SECRET EXHIBITION: Six California Artists
Sussler, Betsy, ed. BOMB: INTERVIEWS
Takahashi, Mutsuo. SLEEPING SINNING FALLING
Turyn, Anne, ed. TOP TOP STORIES
Tutuola, Amos. FEATHER WOMAN OF THE JUNGLE
Tutuola, Amos. SIMBI & THE SATYR OF THE DARK JUNGLE
Valaoritis, Nanos. MY AFTERLIFE GUARANTEED
VandenBroeck, André. BREAKING THROUGH
Veltri, George. NICE BOY
Waldman, Anne. FAST SPEAKING WOMAN
Wilson, Colin. POETRY AND MYSTICISM
Wilson, Peter Lamborn. SACRED DRIFT
Wynne, John. THE OTHER WORLD
Zamora, Daisy. RIVERBED OF MEMORY